Student Research for Community Change

Student Research for Community Change

Tools to Develop Ethical Thinking and Analytic Problem Solving

William Tobin
Valerie Feit

TEACHERS COLLEGE PRESS

TEACHERS COLLEGE | COLUMBIA UNIVERSITY
NEW YORK AND LONDON

Published by Teachers College Press,® 1234 Amsterdam Avenue, New York, NY 10027

Copyright © 2020 by Teachers College, Columbia University

Library of Congress Control Number: 2020938976

ISBN 978-0-8077-6380-3 (paper)
ISBN 978-0-8077-6381-0 (hardcover)
ISBN 978-0-8077-7852-4 (ebook)

Printed on acid-free paper
Manufactured in the United States of America

Contents

Preface   **vii**

Acknowledgments   **xiii**

Introduction   **xv**

    What Is Tools for Change?   xv

    Ethical Thinking and Doing and Analytical Problem Solving   xv

    What Is the *TfC* Guide?   xviii

    How to Use the *TfC* Guide   xxiii

    Research = Inquiring with Intention   xxiii

    Assessment Overview   xxvii

TfC RESEARCH STEPS

Step 1.   PERSPECTIVE: **Developing Engaged Perspectives**   **3**

Step 2.   QUESTION: **Identifying and Framing Empirical Research Questions**   **22**

Step 3.   CONVERSATION: **"Conversing" with Other Researchers and Writing a Literature Review**   **35**

Step 4.   DESIGN: **Developing a Plan to Collect Data to Answer a Research Question**   **56**

Step 5.   DATA: **Researching with Integrity: Ethical Data Collection**   **71**

Step 6.   ANALYSIS: **Analyzing Data to Answer a Research Question**   **90**

Step 7.   IMPLEMENTATION: **Putting New Knowledge to Use**   **106**

Postscript   **127**

Appendix A: Self-Assessment Rubric   **128**

Appendix B: Seeing and Being Rubric   **131**

Appendix C: Team Leadership Rubric   **133**

Notes   **134**

Index   **137**

About the Authors   **142**

Preface

The European newspaper editors, government officials, nongovernmental organization (NGO) leaders, and social entrepreneurs recognized that the Duke University
students they supervised in *DukeEngage Dublin*[1] possessed an ethical and analytical
method for framing and solving problems. Local government officials and community leaders have identified the same method in the Tools for Change high
school students they have worked with across the United States. Tools for Change
(*TfC*), the name of the method introduced in this book, has been taught for more
than a decade to students of all ages and on two continents.

    TfC in partnership with the Kenan Institute for Ethics at Duke University com-
bines ethical thinking and doing and analytical problem solving in a single inquiry
method. *TfC* teaches middle, high school, and college students to reflect on what
is right, good, and fair and then test their ethical principles by applying social science research methods in their classes and communities. *TfC* grows college-ready
students who possess an ethical and analytical style of citizenship.

    What does "college-ready students who possess an ethical and analytical style
of citizenship" mean back on planet Earth in the standards-based classrooms most
of us teach in? Precisely because *TfC* is a method, it plays well with the curriculum
in your classroom and the standards that shape the school day. First, *TfC* redefines
what student participation and classroom activities mean and connects them directly to objective assessments. In *TfC* classrooms, participation is about short tests
of applied curricular understanding, not just how many times a student speaks.
In *TfC* classrooms, activities are focused on devising interview questions about
the science behind climate change for members of the County's Sustainability
Committee, not creating a slide presentation about clean water. In this way, participation and action are occasions to investigate the curriculum in a manner that
enhances analytical and ethical understanding.

    In addition, and more importantly, *TfC* deepens curricular understanding not
by teaching to the test, but by helping students develop facility with a method
that animates inquiry in college, is the basis for the professions, and informs every
walk of life. *TfC* is designed to remind us that meeting standards should be a
means to an end; a means to prepare our students to bring new knowledge—that
is, skills and information—to bear on the most pressing challenges in their lives.

This guide is an effort to realize the aspiration behind *TfC*. Running throughout the pages that follow is the conviction that all our students can learn this method within the existing structures and curriculum of today's middle and high schools (and colleges) and in a manner that is respectful of the works and lives of teachers. This book represents one "try" at helping teachers do what everyone in U.S. education says is necessary: Strike a balance between meeting standards and innovating so that we can grow inclusive groups of young people who are capable of collaborating to address adaptive challenges.

Striking this balance requires that we look backward as well as forward, adapting the humility necessary to learn from our best traditions and the boldness necessary to innovate; leaning into the arduous, but essential, work of face-to-face relationship building as well as the facility to make instant, virtual connections. We contend that a student-driven approach that combines the old and the new is the only way to do this wildly difficult work. Indeed, we are convinced that this kind of informal, pragmatic, bottom-up movement provides the best hope for educational change in the United States. What is needed are wise, innovative, collaborative curricular models that are anchored in the lives of teachers, their students, and the communities they live in.

We don't call, then, for a top-down approach to our educational challenges. We don't introduce another idiosyncratic problem-solving curriculum with special language that only makes sense in the K–12 world. Nor, do we call for a new kind of teacher, student, parent, or school day. Instead, we offer an ethical and analytical style of problem solving that fits the enduring grammar of schooling in the United States. In one form or another, social scientific methods undergird analysis and inquiry in virtually every realm of our society from childcare to management consulting and everything in between. In many of these professions, this method is accompanied by ethical codes of conduct. Moreover, these methods are still and always necessarily becoming, awaiting new problems, fresh perspectives, and new forms of innovation and creativity.

This method is so ubiquitous and so imbedded in our heads we don't recognize it as a research method at all. In its most basic form, it is the process we all use to address challenges in our lives in and out of school. The taken-for-granted character of this problem-solving style suggests both why we need to help our students be self-conscious of it as early in their educational careers as possible and why all teachers can teach and model this method.

Our students illustrate what this method looks like in real life. James was one of Bill's *DukeEngage Dublin* students. He worked with unaccompanied minors in a state school in Dublin. These young people ranged in age from 14 to 18 and had arrived in Dublin from virtually every continent via the most circuitous and emotionally painful paths imaginable. The professional group that James worked with was a tight-knit, down-to-earth group of teachers, social workers, and therapists. In his first few weeks at the school, James focused on understanding the family-like culture the staff had created for their students. He did such a good job of becoming part of this "family" that eventually he was able to see pressing, yet unarticulated needs in the school.

One of these needs centered on the profound difficulties a few of the older male students were having in the school. Like so many of their classmates, these young men had recently arrived in Ireland with no family and no medical history. They were also extremely guarded. When James watched these students, he started making connections between how they were responding to their new environment and the behavioral characteristics of young people who had spectrum disorders (which he had encountered while serving as an intern the previous summer in a Michigan hospital) and/or experienced trauma in childhood, a not uncommon occurrence among separated or refugee young people.

With this previous experience in mind, James continued to observe the students and then, in consultation with his supervisor, but with no fanfare, he started adapting some of the simple, nonclinical behavioral interventions that research suggested would help relieve the extreme agitation these young people experienced regardless of the source. For example, he created some quiet, dark, but safe environments that the young men could retreat to when they were distressed. Almost immediately, these interventions proved to be remarkably effective in providing comfort to the students. Shortly thereafter, James was asked to collaborate with the care team that was responsible for developing a formal intervention plan for the young men; a remarkable and unprecedented sign of the trust the team had in him. At the same time, James developed on his own initiative, a simple protocol to help the staff identify students who might be suffering from spectrum disorders and/or childhood trauma and a checklist of simple interventions they might try.

Kevin and Sonia, two of Valerie's students at Rye Neck High School in New York, had exposure to *TfC* before they were assigned a task called a "critical lens" in their English class. Based on Charles Dickens' *A Tale of Two Cities*, the critical lens assignment entailed writing detailed character and plot analyses and multiple short essays that the students knew had formulaic answers. Frustrated with the way the richness of the novel was being dumbed down to enable students to practice writing essays on a Regents exam,[2] Sonia told Valerie that she viewed the critical lens assignment as the equivalent of "filling out insurance forms."

This gave Valerie an idea for a short social science experiment that would deepen Sonia and Kevin's experience with the critical lens assignment. In another class, the students had read about the increasing trend toward outsourcing work overseas. "Why not," Valerie wondered, "let's see what would happen if they 'outsourced' this assignment." By overlaying what would have been a conventional 20th-century school exercise with an experiment designed to understand what globalization means for individuals, Sonia and Kevin moved from dread to excitement.

After receiving permission from Dr. Barbara Ferraro, Rye Neck High School's progressive principal, Valerie engaged the services of "Andrew," an online assistant who worked in Bangalore for *My Man in India*. Sonia and Kevin emailed Andrew to explain what was needed to complete the critical lens assignment for *A Tale of Two Cities*. They forwarded resources including previous classroom handouts, Spark Notes, commentaries written by English literature scholars, work samples, and instructions for him. When Sonia and Kevin received the initial work product from Andrew, they realized that they would have to incentivize him if they wanted to get his best work.

Valerie suggested that they read Daniel Pink's book, *Drive*, which focuses on motivation research. Sonia and Kevin noticed that Pink had shared his email address on the back cover and they contacted him. Mr. Pink advised the students to put time into getting to know Andrew, rather than just send him resources and instructions. The next time they wrote to Andrew, they did not even mention the assignment, rather, they inquired about his life, school experiences, and goals with genuine interest. Subsequent correspondence moved to a more informal and friendly banter that Sonia and Kevin looked forward to. Soon, Andrew was advancing his own ideas to make the assignment better.

Ultimately, Sonia and Kevin spent more time on *A Tale of Two Cities* than they otherwise might have, and the experiment taught them that globalization may well depend on genuine human connections. They presented their modest findings to classmates, and this knowledge has informed the way they have engaged with globalization in college and now in their work lives. Sonia and Kevin are only two of the many *TfC* graduates who have gone on to colleges and universities where they have told us their thinking and actions continue to be substantially influenced by the confidence and resourcefulness that they gained through their high school *TfC* research experiences.

We tell these stories to highlight the ways James, Sonia, and Kevin engaged with people and situations—that is, their problem-solving style. This style has two primary characteristics. First, the decision to engage came largely from within these students. James, Sonia, and Kevin didn't wait for someone to tell them there was a problem or something didn't make sense. While James had a formal work plan at the school, it certainly did not include understanding and addressing the behavior of the boys. Indeed, no one told him to fully lean into the life of the school. Similarly, Sonia and Kevin decided not to do the easy thing of mindlessly completing an assignment simply because it was assigned. However, once the decision was made to engage, it was possible to see puzzles that needed to be explored. Why were the boys acting as they did? Is globalization just a set of transactions?

Second, the students approached their puzzles in a manner that was informal *even while it* had a discernible, logical structure. Once he identified the problem, James was not reading from a detailed, step-by-step manual on how to respond to separated children who may have spectrum disorders. Yet, his thinking and doing was far from idiosyncratic. Indeed, on closer examination, one can recognize a very familiar social science research methodology in the actions of James, Sonia, and Kevin.

- Engagement: "This doesn't make sense."
- Framing a problem.
- Surveying existing knowledge for ideas on how to address the problem.
- Testing these ideas with a real-life experiment.
- Bringing new knowledge and ideas to bear on the original problem.

The three students didn't put on lab coats, announce that they were doing research, and produce a formal research paper. Instead, they internalized an ethical and analytical method as a part of their personal style and employed this style to address challenges in their lives.

It is tempting to believe that only our best students or children of privilege can develop this informal logical problem-solving style. But, the ability and willingness to engage and empathize can't be measured by an SAT test, bought, or inherited. These qualities come from within a student. They can be encouraged, developed, and refined through practice in the real world. This book demonstrates that the ability to internalize the social science problem-solving method can also result from experiences in school or in the community, if those experiences are designed to promote a collaborative style that places responsibility for both process and outcome on the learner and assessments are based on real-world standards.

The *TfC* method is inspired by three undergraduate programs at Duke University that Bill has co-created and taught with Suzanne Shanahan: The Citizenship Lab at the Kenan Institute for Ethics, *DukeEngage Dublin*, and the Honors Program in Sociology. Additionally, Bill's perspective was informed by a range of educational experiences including undertaking community research projects with migrant and refugee second-level students in Europe; teaching rural, suburban, and urban high school students in America from every achievement stratum, racial, and economic background; and leading teams of university and underserved high school students in community settings. Valerie has used the Schoolwide Enrichment Model[3] (SEM) to create a project-based inquiry curriculum animated by the *TfC* method that spans the middle and high school years in the Rye Neck School District.

Taken together, these experiences have convinced us that *all* students can learn to empathetically, informally, and systematically do evidence-based problem solving. Moreover, as James's story illustrates, community-based problem solving will only be successful if it is done in collaboration with people whose perspectives reflect the diversity in our schools and the world beyond. Put differently, an informal, collaborative, disciplinary-based problem-solving style doesn't make sense unless all our students can make it their own.

Our overlapping experiences in universities and high schools has also convinced us that life is too short to waste another second waiting for state legislatures,

school leaders, blue ribbon standards committees, and college admissions directors to realize that preparation for college and university—to narrow it to that
for a moment—must include *at least some* student experiences with ethical and
analytical thinking and doing and practice bringing knowledge to bear on challenges they care about. This work cannot safely wait until students get to college.
Colleges and universities are simply too loosely coupled to assume that this learning will naturally happen when students get to campus. The only way students
learn how to think and take action in a method is by actually doing disciplinary-
based collaborative thinking and doing. The students are up for this challenge.
The question is: Are the adults?

Acknowledgments

Tobin: I have been lucky enough to work on Tools for Change research with hundreds of incredible young people on two continents over more than a decade. I hope that their intelligence, commitment, and persistence come through in the pages of this book. Thanks also to the teachers, administrators, government officials, NGO leaders, and donors who have helped us grow Tools for Change: Town of Rye, New York, Greg Arcaro, Joe and Roz Carvin, Mitchell Combs, Debbie Reisner, David and Joan Thomas, Mildred Weissman, Jack Zaccara, Sheri Zarkower, the League of Women Voters of Rye, Rye Brook, and Port Chester and the Westchester County Youth Bureau. In Newark, New Jersey, Diane Hill, Habeebah Yasin, Maxine Sumney, Shanice Thomas, and Chancellor Nancy Cantor at Rutgers University-Newark. In North Carolina, Jennifer Allen, Martine Aurelien, Dawn Blankenship, Patrick Brashears, Tiara Fennell, Susan Hines, Karili Mikula, Jennifer McBrayer, Frank McKay, Rhonda Medford Maurice Nicholson, Katrine Rathe, and Marla Webber. In Dublin, Ireland, Alex Klein and Miatta Echetebu.

Long ago, Marc Ventresca showed me that it was possible to inhabit a research method as a way of being in the world every day. Charlie Kurzman carefully read and made valuable comments on an earlier draft of this book.

Together Suzanne Shanahan and I designed and taught the Duke programs that inspired the Tools for Change method, she helped me understand that ethics and analysis could be joined, and over the years she supported Tools for Change in ways small and large. Thanks, Suzanne, for all of this and everything else.

Feit: Thank you to Rye Neck School District Superintendent of Schools, Dr. Barbara Ferraro, for her professional and personal support. Thanks to former Superintendent of Schools, Dr. Peter Mustich, Rye Neck Middle School Principal and Assistant Superintendent for Instruction, Dr. Eric Lutinski, and the successive Board of Education Trustees who have shaped Rye Neck's vibrant learning community. Thank you to Linda Costelloe, high school librarian, who has instilled a research mindset in our students and is as passionate about student research as we are. Thanks to principals Marge Longabucco, Michael Scarantino, Dr. Tina Wilson, and Tara Goldberg for your educational program support. Appreciation goes to Leigh Ann Kowalchik-Porphy, William McKeon, Kelly Addorisio, Jessie Vega, and Katherine Offner, the teachers whose dedication to inquiry has animated the curiosity of thousands of children.

Thanks to John Dalton for support and advice. Thanks to Scott Beall, a visionary educator who inspires my journey. Meka, it is your future that I always have in mind.

Introduction

WHAT IS TOOLS FOR CHANGE?

This guide is designed to make it easy to teach *all* our students to do ethical and analytical inquiry in their daily lives in and out of school. The guide builds on years of reflective practice and is intended to make it easy for educators to teach their students to do ethical, social science inquiry by providing instruction, support, and resources. The guide illustrates how to transform student participation and classroom activities into individual and collaborative inquiries into the curriculum you are using now so that students can demonstrate mastery of the curriculum as they build research skills and mindsets that prepare them for the future.

ETHICAL THINKING AND DOING AND ANALYTICAL PROBLEM SOLVING

Tools for Change *(TfC)* with the Kenan Institute for Ethics and Duke University grows college-ready students who possess an ethical and analytical style of citizenship. This style is a way for students *to be* in their classrooms and in the world beyond the school. *TfC* combines moral behavior and reasoning with analytical problem solving, ethics, and empirical research.

The most urgent and pressing challenges that concern us invariably have a critical, but unexplored, ethical dimension. To ask how we allocate scarce resources—like places in our "best" colleges—is also to raise questions about what is fair? Inquiring if humans should be cloned is also to wonder about what is right and wrong. Asking how much we should pay in taxes is also a query about justice. To wonder what kind of school or community we want is also to ask what good means.

The *TfC* guide introduces ethical thinking and doing as three components of the method we use to address and bring knowledge to bear on challenges. These three components offer teachers discretion and flexibility in how they combine ethics and research in their classrooms:

1. *as perspective.* Some patterns are difficult to identify because they are so rare; others are hard to spot because they are so common. Seeing what is

right, just, and fair is challenging precisely because "ethics is everywhere." *TfC* helps teachers highlight the ethical dimension within the curriculum and the world outside the school. (People working in the field of ethics call this "descriptive ethics.")

2. *as reasoning.* How do we decide what is good, just, and fair and how do we explain this to ourselves and those in our classrooms and communities? Ethical reasoning should not be an abstract mental activity that occurs only in the heads of our students or solely in response to invented hypotheticals. *TfC* helps teachers use the puzzles, problems, and questions that exist in the curriculum and the community to guide their students through the process by which they decide what they believe to be ethical and come to understand the beliefs of others. (People working in the field of ethics call this "applied ethics.")

3. *as obligation.* How do we convey to students the ethical obligations that are woven into the fabric of everyday life, without telling them how to be good or to repeat the imperative to "make good choices," whatever that means? *TfC* helps teachers introduce their students to the duties that researchers assume by virtue of being researchers and have committed themselves to upholding. (People working in the field of ethics also call this "applied ethics.")

In *TfC*, ethical seeing, reasoning, and obligation are indispensable aspects of the inquiry process: for defining our most pressing problems, deciding what data is required to get fresh leverage on them, how to collect and analyze data, and, finally, how to generate the consensus necessary to implement even the best evidence-based recommendations.

The ability to think and act ethically and engage analytically enables *TfC* students to enrich concepts in biology and add depth to issues in U.S. history every day in classrooms around the country. *TfC* students and their teachers have also used the method to bring new knowledge to bear on problems in their schools and communities.

TfC is a method that students internalize as a go-to way of being in the world—methods are about *thinking and doing* in a structured way. Curriculum, on the other hand, is essential as a way for teachers to deliver information to students—curriculum is *learning about*. *TfC* makes it possible to flexibly add ethical and analytical thinking and doing to this learning.

The *TfC* Method and Student Online Engagement

TfC utilizes the Internet as a means to more efficiently converse with our students and other researchers (through the use of online databases in Step 3) and collect data (through the use of online surveys in Steps 4–5). In *TfC*, the Internet is both a resource and tool that, when used judiciously, supports but does not supplant active engagement with people and direct experiences in classrooms interactively online (Google Meets, Zoom) or on the ground in a community setting. In fact, engagement with the *TfC* method provides students with a significantly different experience than the ones they typically have online. In this way, the *TfC* method complements and augments students' online engagement in two important ways.

1. The *TfC* method begins with the assumption that our most vexing adaptive challenges require the ability to converse, to forge respectful face-to-face relationships, and to think and do in our three-dimensional world. The medium of the Internet is designed for conversation and discourse at scale. The ability for (almost) all of us to take positions and have an opinion is an incredibly recent advance and one not to be taken for granted. However, discourse at scale is not the same thing as, nor can it be a substitute for, problem solving in the classroom or community. Students need to be able to do both. They need to be able to talk about morality and test their own moral principles in their neighborhoods and practice living up to ethical obligations.

2. The Internet defines, strengthens, and elaborates individual and group identities. In the *TfC* method, a sense of identity is important in helping to shape the perspectives by which students see the world, identify what doesn't make sense, and define the challenges they want to address. However, the success of the research process depends on the ability of students to also—to the extent possible—bound or bracket their own perspective so they can respectfully see, hear, and understand those with other perspectives.

The *TfC* Method and Existing Experiential, Civic, Inquiry, and Project-Based Learning Programs

TfC can be distinguished from other experiential, inquiry, and citizenship curriculums in four crucial ways:

1. *TfC is designed for all students*. All students can learn ethical thinking and doing and analytical problem solving. Indeed, the success of *TfC* inquiry depends on diverse and inclusive classrooms.

2. *TfC combines research and citizenship so students can bring knowledge to bear on the most important challenges facing them*. *TfC* does not artificially and arbitrarily separate ethics and analysis or research and citizenship. Nor does it disaggregate the research method into discrete standards. Instead, it integrates these enterprises in a manner that reflects the way students will encounter them in their lives within and outside of school.

3. *TfC was developed in a university and then field tested for over a decade in high schools*. It is designed with years of first-hand knowledge of how college

students actually take advantage of the academic opportunities on campus and help others do the same. It employs this knowledge to grow cohorts of students who can do what we want our best undergraduates to do: contribute to a diverse environment of experimentation, debate, inquiry, and interpretation as they learn to bring knowledge to bear on our most pressing human challenges. *TfC* is a method that connects K–12 to college and career in an organic and substantive manner. Indeed, in one form or another, the research method taught in *TfC* animates dozens of college and university majors and is the basis for inquiry and problem solving in most careers, professions, and industries.

4. *TfC works with and complements curriculum that teachers are already using. TfC* does not ask teachers and administrators to choose it over the curriculums they are already using. The *TfC* guide is deliberately designed to make it easy to bring ethical thinking and doing and analytical problem solving to the social studies (*TfC* is an example of how empirical data can be used with the C3 Inquiry Arc) and STEM curriculum as well as experiential and inquiry-based curriculum such as project-based learning (PBL) and service learning.

WHAT IS THE *TfC* GUIDE?

The *TfC* guide contains:

- An overview of the seven distinct steps in the social science inquiry method complete with case studies, field-tested strategies, and examples of how to plan and teach these steps as stand-alone lessons or as part of a sequenced inquiry process.
- Teacher-created resources—lessons, lectures, activities, worksheets—to illustrate the specific skills, techniques, and mindsets contained within each distinct step.
- A guide for assessing student learning in the *TfC* method, along with examples of formative and summative assessment for each step and the method as a whole
- Strategies for integrating the *TfC* inquiry method with curriculum and experiential and inquiry-based learning programs that are presently in your classroom and school.

The Design of the *TfC* Guide

The guidebook is organized around the seven discrete but related steps in the social science research method and the learning objectives and learning skills that are associated with these inquiry steps. These steps are presented here in sequence. By following these steps, the method can be taught in its entirety. These steps are also separate elements in the inquiry process with distinct learning goals, skills, and mindsets. The steps illustrate different ways research can enrich and deepen the curriculum. Each step, therefore, can stand alone and can be independently integrated into existing curriculum.

Steps in the *TfC* Method

1. PERSPECTIVE. Developing Engaged Perspectives

   Learning Goals[1]:
   - Listen to others for verbal and nonverbal content.
   - Respond to an exchange of ideas and beliefs.
   - Offer explanations and remain open to new thinking.
   - Collaborate with diverse team members.

   Thinking and Doing:
   - Reflect on how we decide what is right, good, and fair.
   - Identify the principles that guide these beliefs.
   - Undertake personal inventories and self-assessments to better understand the perspectives of classmates.
   - Recognize the value of an inclusive research team for the work of inquiry.

2. QUESTION. Identifying and Framing Empirical Research Questions

   Learning Goals:
   - Use individual perspectives to identify issues of concern and angles of leverage.
   - Engage in problem finding and framing as a precondition for problem solving.

   Thinking and Doing:
   - Surface the ethical dimension of political, historical, and scientific content and community challenges.
   - Define research questions so they can be answered with new data.
   - Identify puzzles and problems in curriculum by analyzing "what doesn't make sense."

3. CONVERSATION. "Conversing" with Other Researchers, Field Experts, and Government Officials in the Creation of a Literature Review

   Learning Goals:
   - Apply prior empirical research to support arguments.
   - Synthesize information and beliefs from multiple perspectives.
   - Develop a point of view.

Thinking and Doing:
- Read and assess scholarly articles.
- Mine databases, comparing and contrasting arguments, methods, and evidence.
- Synthesize information from multiple perspectives.
- Evaluate sources of information.

4. DESIGN. Developing a Plan to Collect New Data to Find Answers to Research Questions

Learning Goals:
- Define and understand disciplinary concepts, vocabulary, and terms of use.
- Project design and management.
- Design and piloting of qualitative instruments—such as surveys.

Thinking and Doing:
- Compare and contrast the relative merits of competing data collection methods.
- Develop skills to create effective surveys, focus group prompts, and interview questions and techniques.

5. DATA COLLECTION. Researching with Integrity: Ethical Data Collection

Learning Goals:
- Collaborate with research team members.
- Learn basic statistical concepts and skills and understand how to assess risk in research involving human subjects.

Thinking and Doing:
- Administer a survey.
- Conduct a focus group and or interviews.
- Convey the balance of risks and benefits to subjects.
- Respectfully and consistently communicate with research subjects regarding their participation.
- Manage the social and technical logistics of data collection.

6. ANALYSIS. Analyzing Data to Find Answers to Research Questions

Learning Goals:
- Group and order information/data.
- Identify themes and patterns in qualitative data.
- Observe, ask questions, and develop associations between behaviors, phenomenon, and patterns.
- Recognize sources of bias in research.

Thinking and Doing:
- Make associations and develop meanings based on data that are relevant to research question or curricular problem or puzzle.

- Analyze survey, focus group, and interview data by employing field-tested method of analysis—such as coding.

7. IMPLEMENTATION. Putting New Knowledge to Use

Learning Goals:

- Communicate through persuasive writing, formal presentations, and through a variety of media.
- Embrace creativity as a means to develop new ideas.
- Understand the limits of data to persuade.
- Collaborate with field experts, community leaders, and organizations.
- Identify audiences and constituencies.

Thinking and Doing:

- Develop evidence-based and ethical arguments that advance policy recommendations and solutions.
- Identify appropriate audiences and constituencies.
- Produce persuasive research reports and presentations.
- Find mentors, and build partnerships, consulting relationships, and collaborations to disseminate and implement.

How to Apply *TfC* Inquiry Steps

Each step in the *TfC* inquiry is organized to ensure the flexibility and ease of use required to realize learning goals, undertake activities, and use reflection in today's classrooms.

Each discrete inquiry step features the following user-friendly sections[2]:

- Introduction
- Case Study
- Key Features
- Planning
- Teaching
- Assessment (of student learning and understanding)
- Frequently Asked Questions
- eToolBox—links to ideas, activities, blacklines, work samples, and other resources

Tools for Change in Schools, Colleges, and Communities

Tools for Change has been successfully used:

- In middle and high schools.
- In interdistrict community programs for high school students.

- In university-based precollege programs for socioeconomically, geographically, and racially diverse student populations.
- With college students in the classroom and in internships.

The *TfC* method has been used to address:

- Challenge of engaging students in remote learning.
- School-based issues such as safety.
- A need for student-voice in the adoption of school policies.
- Infusing science research with ethical perspectives.
- Relevant issues in social studies classes.
- Community-based social issues such as hunger, water quality, transportation, violence, migration, and resettlement, and access to housing, transportation, and medical services.
- Curricular differentiation needs.
- Project-based and service-learning ventures in a manner that supports college and career-readiness goals.

Thus far, middle and high school teachers have taught *TfC* inquiry in three primary ways:

1. Curricular integration of relevant *TfC* steps, skills, mindsets, activities, and/or resources.
2. As a semester or yearlong community research project offered as a component of an elective or seminar.
3. Integrated within experiential and inquiry-based learning projects to introduce depth, relevance, and an ethical dimension.

What Is *TfC* Curricular Integration?

Teach specific inquiry steps:
1. Introduce ethical thinking, doing, and analytical problem solving.
2. Provide opportunities for students to directly engage in a respectful inquiry process that brings new knowledge to bear on the questions and issues that matter to them and to their communities.

TfC Curricular integration in the content classroom:
- English (ELA) classes converse with other researchers and experts (*TfC* Step 2) in order to do college-level research.
- Biology classes learn ethical reasoning (*TfC Thinking and Doing*) to understand the full implications of cloning.
- Students undertake group or individual research projects that align with curricular content.

- Students undertake individual research projects in talent development programs that emphasize student choice and the development of strengths and interests.

TfC College and Career Preparation Seminars and Electives:
- Structure a college and career preparation seminar based on the *TfC* method or devote one day each week in such a seminar to a *TfC* school or community project.
- Offer an elective class based on *TfC* methods with a focus on a shared project that leads to smaller group or individual research.

TfC in Project-Based Learning (PBL), Service-Learning Projects (SLP), and in Community Centers:
- Youth groups use the entire *TfC* method to address school or community challenges.
- Students develop their ethical and analytical perspectives (*TfC* Step 1) to get the most out of a project-based learning (PBL) unit on conservation.
- Students in a PBL or SLP class use steps in the *TfC* method to address school or community challenges as a group and/or develop individual research projects that align with school priorities and/or student interests.
- Student members of a school improvement team use the *TfC* method to address dangerous behavior in school restrooms.

HOW TO USE THE *TfC* GUIDE

For integration into curriculum or within experiential, civic, inquiry, or project-based learning programs, browse through the book and begin with the steps that interest you most.

For semester or yearlong community research projects: Examine the table of contents and read Step 7 to understand where the research might culminate and then read sequentially through the steps.

RESEARCH = INQUIRING WITH INTENTION

Many students and teachers believe that social studies research is about downloading articles from the Internet and then answering questions that have right or wrong answers. This idea of research is so deeply ingrained that even students who attend universities such as Duke—institutions whose very reason for being is connected to the research enterprise—arrive on campus with little or no interest in research (and/or understanding of what research is).

Social science research that occurs outside of the K–12 setting has little to do with moving information from one screen to another or filling in the blanks. This is especially true of the most exciting social science research, empirical research, which is the focus of the *TfC* method and involves collecting new evidence to answer a question. Research is inquiry. More precisely, research is *self-conscious or intentional* investigation. All of us inquire and investigate every day in a manner that is so natural that we are not even aware we are doing it. It is easier to see what research actually is, why it is worth doing, and the fact that all of us can do it, when research is connected back to everyday inquiry.

We often start our work with high school students with an everyday inquiry story from Bill's life:

One morning, I woke up and a bike that I had recently bought was missing from my porch. I started by wondering whether finding out who stole the bike was the right question. Did I leave my bike at Jason's house after another last second loss by my beloved Philadelphia 76ers had left me— once again—dazed and confused? When I was sure I wasn't dealing with brain freeze, my investigation began in earnest. First, I tried to find out if the neighbors saw anything, then I made a police report, then I tried to find out if there were other reports of bikes stolen in and around our house in recent days, and finally I spoke to people about how best to find a stolen bike.

Then, armed with this information, I developed a strategy to find my bike by first driving around the neighborhood looking for the bike; then, I examined the bike "pound" at the police station; and, finally, I posted a reward for the bike on telephone poles around the neighborhood. When these strategies were not successful, I concluded the bike was probably gone for good. So, I integrated what I learned into my future behavior: after this experience, I always locked my bike, brought it inside every night, and registered the serial number so that it could be tracked if it ever went missing again. Then, I turned the page.

Inquiry happens when people try to find lost bikes, when a group of social workers have an hour to sit around a conference table in the Durham County Department of Social Services to brainstorm next steps in their most difficult cases, when a team at McKinsey Consulting prepares a report for a client, or when two sociologists realize what they learned in their research as they finish the first draft of an article for a respected journal.

Bill and the social workers in Durham, the consultants in Dubai, and the professors in a university all followed a similar process of inquiry, a process that corresponds to the method in this book, and looks like this:

1. Determine the scope of a situation.
2. Develop a question to focus attention and perhaps develop a hypothesis.

3. Find out what others who have looked at a similar question know.
4. Collect data to get new leverage on the question.
5. Analyze the data.
6. Bring the new knowledge acquired through inquiry to bear on the problem.

In the past, we might have said that the inquiry undertaken by sociologists is the "high form" and Bill's search for his bike is a recognizable, but dumbed-down version for regular people. But many of those who practice the "high form" no longer think that is quite true. As University of Pennsylvania Professor Philip Tetlock, Investor Ray Dalio, and Nobel Prize winning economist Daniel Kahneman have argued, many kinds of analyses are best carried out by thoughtful, reflective people who are eager to learn and are willing to be surprised. The difference between inquiry and research is not technical proficiency or a PhD; it is, instead, intention. In forecasting future events, understanding how people really act, and in addressing a community challenge, regular people are capable of learning to do research everyday if they are self-conscious about what they are doing.

Inquiring intentionally allows teachers and students alike to become researchers: able and willing to self-consciously adopt an inquiry mindset when needed, identify distinctive steps in the process, and deliberately focus on and refine skills and techniques.

Lab Roles, Organization, and Expectations

Over the years, we have developed classroom practices that make it easier for teachers to integrate *TfC* methods into their curriculum and for students to do research. Some environments are simply more conducive to inquiry and investigation than others. In as much as it is possible, we try to create a lab environment. In this way, *TfC* seeks to replicate the social environment and expectations that students will encounter in college and in career settings. Whether in a full *TfC* program or a curricular application, we create a research lab that focuses on authentic engagement in relevant work. When students care about the work they are doing, the environment naturally takes on a purposeful "feel." In this environment, being a good lab member doesn't mean being the best at figuring out what the teacher wants or memorizing information to raise a grade-point average. Rather, earning the respect of the members of the lab and being valued for both one's ideas and active contributions to the work at hand are what receive affirmation. It is, as James, Kevin, and Sonia's stories in the *Preface* illustrate, about addressing puzzles, problems, or challenges that matter and doing what is fair, just, and right. Moving students from a checklist, learn-and-test mindset to being a contributing member of a *TfC* team is not as difficult as it sounds. Indeed, we have found that most students want to be a part of something that is worth their time, and they welcome the opportunity be part of a team in which they are taken seriously.

A Seeing and Being Research Mindset

We have found that a slight shift in mindset on the part of the teacher, adopting what we call a *Seeing and Being Research Mindset*, and the adoption of a few flexible strategies that reset the stage for learning goes a long way toward establishing a learning environment that is collaborative, and energized by ideas and a shared responsibility for getting work done. Creating conditions that are more conducive to performing this work and are developmentally appropriate starts with a thoughtful but *not* a time-consuming process.

In *TfC* classrooms, there are three behavioral objectives that are consistently emphasized because we want students to internalize them as habits. They are:

1. Accountability toward self and others.
2. The development of professional behaviors, including living up to a professional code of conduct.
3. An understanding of what it means to produce knowledge and ideas that can be of use to others.

Ultimately, we want students to demand accountability from themselves and positive, productive behaviors from one another.

Research Facilitation

A lab structure builds teamwork and leadership capacities. In the lab, teachers assume roles as lead researchers and work side-by-side with novice student researchers. The teacher is not standing and delivering in this environment; she is instead leading by directing the research process from within. The transfer from the sage-on-the-stage to the guide-on-the-side requires, first and foremost, the ability to facilitate the research process for the class; that is, shaping the investigation so that it has integrity *and* conforms to time and resource constraints. The teacher does this by:

1. Selecting materials, readings, and speakers.
2. *Curating* and circumscribing the process—for example, how much time the students spend on each step if undertaking the entire *TfC* research method—and most importantly, *discerning* what role she needs to play at each stage in the process.
3. *Contributing* work product and *mentoring*.

This facilitation role means that sometimes the teacher may have to write a first draft of the survey questions, sometimes she will decide on the method students will use, and sometimes she will limit the choices provided to students. These are the roles that help ensure that the lab produces quality work, while young researchers gain experience.

Teachers have lots of practice at this kind of facilitation and curation and the guide and the *TfC* website provide examples of how *TfC* teachers have:

1. Curated the research process.
2. Integrated discrete methods, strategies, and skills.
3. Introduced materials that can be tailored to assist in this work.

In a *TfC* classroom, this curation and facilitation sounds like this:

- "Based on our discussion, I want to share a first draft I have written of our introduction. What do you think?"
- "Here are some survey questions that have worked in other places; let's try to understand why they were effective."
- "Let's work together on your script so that people will be more willing to take our survey."
- "Ethical reflection is about being honest, not being right."

In a *TfC* lab, students are simply expected to ask questions about all aspects of the process and actively work to earn the respect of their teachers and peers. Expectations extend to the details of *how* and *what* each student contributes to group conversations and even to the expressions they have on their faces while listening to others speak. Meeting deadlines and responding promptly to email and online communication are as important to individual and lab success as is mastery of the method.

Teams

Where appropriate, teamwork and leadership are communicated through a tiered structure that connects students by placing them on teams with rotating student leaders.

Teams are formed before work begins, rather than assigning students to groups after the fact and only to fulfill an assignment. With a combination of explicit behavioral expectations and an engaging method that directly connects students to the real world in a structured manner, we have managed to help students overcome the malaise that comes from doing assignments and tests that are ends in themselves—they are, that is, disassociated from the outside world—or are simply thrown into the trash after a grade is earned because of their lack of relevance to where students want to go next.

ASSESSMENT OVERVIEW

How do we respectfully stretch, coax, and cajole well-established student evaluation practices that have been used to assess content mastery so they support the development of research thinking and doing?

TfC assessment is focused on how to:

- Frame research questions.
- Converse with other researchers and community members.
- Use the social science research method to collect new data.
- Analyze and identify patterns in data.
- Bring new knowledge to bear on challenges and problems.

TfC emphasizes formative assessment and evidence about:

1. Where students (as individuals and as members of a research team) are in relation to meeting desired learning objectives and outcomes.
2. The effectiveness of the teacher in helping students reach this result.

TfC is essentially a method, a verb, waiting to be put to use to enable students to handle open-ended questions, problems, puzzles, and challenges in a variety of curricular contexts and in the larger world.

Curricular Assessment Models and *TfC* Assessment

Research is a social process. It builds on the work of previous researchers and is intended to be used by people in the world. Similarly, we have learned much about assessment from recent work that redefines understanding as an active verb, specifically, performance—for example, *Teaching for Understanding* and *Understanding by Design*. This exciting work focused on active "understanding" is animated by curricular needs. However, *TfC* is not a curriculum, but instead a method. Put simply, *Teaching for Understanding* and *Understanding by Design* require a different kind of teacher and student stretch than *TfC*. Helping students demonstrate performative understanding requires that teachers stretch in terms of how they understand and teach the curriculum; the flexibility is, if you will, confined to the world of K–12. "Essential questions" are critical but they are, in the last analysis, answerable within the curriculum. Performances make clear that students have understood—in the broad, but not imprecise way this word is used—the curriculum.[3]

The stretch for most *TfC* teachers and students is to straddle the worlds of high school and college *and*—this is a big "and"—to do this stretching in a middle or high school environment. So, we seek to inform high school assessment practices with an understanding of what relevant college assessment looks like. Then, we can tweak high school assessment practices so they capture the best college-level thinking and doing *and* still be doable for teachers.

TfC reasoning, analysis, and problem solving are necessarily open-ended journeys because what the researcher will find (besides greater humility) is not clear from the outset. Questions that move beyond critical thinking to more exploratory levels are not bound by the curriculum, however generously defined. Instead, the existing curriculum is used as a resource that can inform the question at hand, as a point of departure for exploring puzzles and questions via analysis and ethical reflection.

The work here, and in college more broadly, is not about learning or moving information. It is about doing a method, seizing opportunities associated with these methods, and contributing to a collaborative environment where these methods are used to bring skills and new ideas to society.

Our aspiration for our students is that they learn in a manner that makes them want to collaboratively "play" the research "game" so they can solve the problems that matter to them most. "Common sense logic," "effective," and "wisdom rooted in experience" are the words that describe the research game *TfC* teaches. They also characterize our approach to assessment.

Formative, Summative, and Performance Assessments in a University Lab or High School Classroom

A university lab features a range of formative assessments and a smaller number of summative assessments all integrated in an organic manner. During their time in a university lab, undergraduates will get frequent and varied feedback from experienced researchers: graduate students, post grads, and the lab director. These assessments are largely informal and are woven into the everyday life of the lab—"This is how you conduct a focus group," "Here are corrections on your draft of the methods section of our article," and "Are you getting the experiences that will help you get to where you want to go next?"

Research is a way of being that isn't grown through command or incentives, but by instruction and modeling, encouragement and feedback, and mentored practice. This is work that is both formal and informal. Here is an informal exchange Bill had with two undergraduates in the Citizenship Lab he directs at Duke:

> The attached article highlights another stream of research that is relevant to our work in the Citizenship Lab: university-based efforts to teach high school students to use research to address a community issue. . . . Here is a possible opening sentence for our literature review: "The Citizenship Lab lies at the intersection of three areas of research and practice: (1) refugee 'resettlement' in America and cross-nationally; (2) college/university preparation programs for underserved high school students; and (3) programs designed to teach high school students research skills to address challenges in their community." Take a look at the article and my draft opening sentence for our literature review section and give me suggestions for making it more effective.

In the Citizenship Lab, summative assessments are robust—such as a memo for the Associate School Superintendent on Translation and Interpretation, a survey of bus riders, an op-ed piece, or a grant proposal to bring an adult-student mentoring program to scale. These performances are graded. But a grade is nominal in the Citizenship Lab and nonexistent in most other lab settings in a university. The real evaluation is a letter of recommendation that testifies to the student's ability to apply their learning and bring knowledge to bear. Does the memo Sara wrote persuade the Director of the City's Department of Transportation to respond to the sense of urgency in the voices of his riders? The letter of recommendation helps students get to where they want and need to go next: summer internship, employment, graduate school, medical school, and so on.

It is relatively easy to provide the kind of formative assessments that go on in a university lab, and it is also easy to give students feedback that acknowledges growth.

Assessment in Middle and High Schools

Here's how these practices inform *TfC* assessment practices in the high school context:

- Use a mix of formative and summative assessments.
- Consider weaknesses in student thinking and find the formative assessments that help develop greater strength.
- Replace some quizzes with reflective, analytic responses to prompts.

We suggest a wide range of formative assessment methods, including:

- Evidence from observation.
- Discussion, interviews, and written conversational feedback.
- Individual journal keeping.
- Self and group assessment rubrics.
- Assessment by community members and research peers—if possible.

The best formative assessments are woven into the fabric of the research itself.

For teachers who are integrating specific steps or skills and mindsets within these steps into the curriculum, we discuss formative and summative assessment within the discussion of each step.

For teachers doing semester or yearlong research projects, we suggest sharing and clarifying the formative and summative criteria that will be used to evaluate student work so that it can be reviewed in class and accessed by students as work progresses.

Formative Assessment Evidence Used in *TfC*

Rationale: Formative assessment needs to be integrated so that students are aware that they are constantly receiving triangulated, actionable, performance improvement data that includes:

- **Self-assessment:** How their behaviors as learners and group members shape the outcomes of their relationships and learning.

- **Teacher assessment:** How a teacher (principal researcher) perceives them as an individual and group member.
- **Quantitative assessment:** How quantitative data on performance measures (tests, quizzes, projects) that are criteria-based and also taken by classmates (comparative data) provide valuable evidence of what is and is not understood.

By including the student in this thinking, students are active contributors in the assessment process itself—reinforcing the think and do mindset we advocate. Additionally, this changes the stamp of approval mindset that is present when a student goes through a standardized process and gets a grade at the end.

In traditional classrooms (and, here we include Advanced Placement [AP] classes) there are performance measures that are predominantly quantitative assessments—that is, tests with a grade attached. A percentage of a final grade might include participation—most often, the student will not find out what that is explicitly based on or know about how they are doing overall until a summative assessment results in a grade at the end of the course. We broaden and deepen what student participation means in ways that deepen performative understanding of the curriculum.

What we suggest is a proactive approach that allows students to take ownership of their assessment process. We include choice in students selecting (at least sometimes) the manner in which they want to be assessed and/or what will be assessed. Performance-based formative assessments should be joined with quantitative and feedback assessments to help each student to use a variety of data points to develop the objectivity necessary to improve as a value-added team member.

- Self-assessment:
  - » Checklists
  - » Rubrics
  - » Checkpoints
  - » Journal entries
- Teacher assessment:
  - » Interview/surveys/reflections on student learning
  - » Drafts of reports and presentations
  - » Individual research journals
  - » Observation and informal discussion
- Tests and quizzes

Summative Assessment Evidence Used in *TfC*

Rationale: Teachers should engage in active thinking and doing, alongside their students. This should occur in the course of the research process and in the assessment of the process. Gathering data about what students know and can do in summative performance of understanding should become an integral part of an improvement process in which teachers shape their practices and place emphasis on concepts and skills to better understand their students. Instead of judging students with a grade at the end of a course, which we find that students rarely understand regardless of the rubric employed, we recommend summative assessments that genuinely reflect a classroom experience and are instructive to both students and teachers. Using triangulated data points in formative assessments (student, teacher, and objective measures) that naturally flow into summative performances of understanding (which can include tests) provides a means to understand student achievement in relation to a teacher's evolving practices.

Suggestions for summative assessments for each step may be found in the discussion of that step below. Summative assessments for semester or yearlong research projects should be presented in context as interim measures that assess individual and class growth in mastering content.

What differentiates summative assessments in a *TfC* classroom is that these measures are shared and evaluated with students as individual and group data. Here are some summative assessments that are relevant for semester or yearlong research projects.

- Community Impact (how and to what degree have new knowledge and skills developed in the research process been brought to bear in the community)
  - Presentation and dissemination of findings
  - Implementation of policy recommendations
    » New partnerships and collaborations
    » Pilot programs
- Teacher-Made and State Tests and Quizzes
- Seeing and Being Rubric (Appendix C)
- Team Leadership Rubric (Appendix D)
- Final Presentations/Reports
- Effectiveness of Implementation Efforts, Step 7
- Individual Research Portfolio. Selected by each student to reflect their best work. A portfolio might include:
  » Table of contents
  » Statement outlining individual perspective
  » Draft research questions
  » Student written sections of report or presentation
  » Materials created to ensure informed consent is obtained from research subjects
  » Survey questions, interview protocols, focus group prompts
  » Record or transcript of interviews conducted or focus groups led
  » Evidence of analysis
  » Documentation, log, or record of conversations with community members, leaders of organizations, and/or government officials regarding implementation of recommendations
  » Examples of outcomes that students contributed to—for example, an op-ed piece in a newspaper

TfC RESEARCH STEPS

Perspective
Developing Engaged Perspectives

"Huh, that's weird." This and statements like it are how research begins. There is nothing new in saying that research begins with a puzzle. What is less generally understood is that what counts as weird, strange, or wrong is rarely obvious or self-evident. What is weird frequently depends on who we are, where we're standing, and how we see the world. Moreover, before we can see what is weird, we have to be open to the possibility of the weird, on the lookout for what doesn't make sense. Finally, we need to fight the impulse to simply shrug our shoulders and move on when we encounter what is weird.

We have found that students often struggle to see challenges that matter to them, until they learn to engage the world in a proactive manner and become self-conscious of their own way of seeing. Step 1 of the *TfC* method focuses on helping students both develop a proactive and engaged stance toward the world and use perspectives to illuminate analytical and ethical challenges.

CASE STUDY

Recently, 25 high school students—most of whom were recently arrived refugees—sat around a circle in a large room in Durham, North Carolina. They were discussing a pressing challenge that they, their older siblings, parents, and friends were experiencing: how to balance education, part-time work, and career preparation. In an earlier class, individual students told the group that making enough money to support a family was their ultimate goal. Bill and the students anticipated a research project in which the students would first develop a survey to find out how their peers and siblings were striking this balance—or if they were even thinking about this balance—then administer the survey, and finally share the results with teachers and administrators in the Career Technical Education (CTE) program in the district and the leaders of workforce development and employment training programs in the city.

Here, in the second meeting of the group, Bill was thinking about how to get the students in the circle to understand that the project wouldn't be successful unless each of them figured out what they could contribute to the work. Personal awareness makes it possible for individuals to contribute their unique perspectives to an investigation—in this case, the work of understanding how young newcomers balance school, work, and career. Bill then spoke about how each person has their own viewpoint, a way of seeing, feeling, knowing, and thinking. These ways of seeing and feeling are shaped by who they are. They, in turn, will determine what they see and do in the future. A productive research team needs a broad range of ways of seeing, feeling, and thinking to be successful. Everyone needs to be able to *see* themselves in community research.

Then, Bill distributed a handout that Nikolay Santos, a Duke undergraduate, developed to help the group surface their perspectives and understand what each individual might bring to the research. The handout looked like this.

> I AM . . .
> Because I am _____, I think _____.
> Because I am _____, I feel _____.
> Because I am _____, I see _____.
> Because I am _____, I know _____.

Bill shared the answers he wrote:

- "Because I am a father, I think about how issues impact families for good and bad."
- "Because I am adopted, I feel grateful, but also anxious."

The students broke up in pairs and completed the "I am" statements as honestly as possible. They were told that everyone's "I am" statement would be different and that Bill would be the only one to see their work, unless they wished to share what they had written, which many students had no hesitation to do. In subsequent *TfC* classes for the school-work-career research project, Bill helped students brainstorm ideas on how their "I am" statements would help them contribute to the research. For example, one student with an older sister "who worked so much she had no time to prepare for the General Education Diploma (GED)" understood the need for educational options that were flexible. Over the course of the project, the students updated and refined their "I am" statements.

The "I am" statements were designed to help students understand what informs and shapes their perspectives. They can also serve to introduce the concept of "bias." Edward T. Hall said, "Culture hides more than it reveals." It is not the individual "I am" statement that develops these understandings—although it may be revelatory to a student to more clearly define the influences on their thinking—the "I am" statements take on a different meaning when they are shared by the students. As differences emerge between students and they learn about what motivates other people's attitudes and actions, they begin to understand who they are and what they, and only they, can contribute to the research process.

KEY FEATURES

Students are more likely to see what doesn't make sense and then act on this in-sight if they possess the ability to engage proactively and develop an awareness of, and capacity to use, their own and others' perspectives.

The ability to adopt an engaged and proactive attitude toward the world is indispensable for research. Research can't begin without a puzzle, a problem, or a question. Only occasionally are these puzzles and problems obvious for all to see. Moreover, the solutions to these problems rarely if ever announce themselves. Instead, researchers must learn to seek out what doesn't make sense or, at the very least, be open to the existence of the crazy and strange. The late writer Toni Morrison read the newspaper each morning with a pencil to more easily correct the errors she knew she would find. This proactive engagement with the world is an attitude or stance all our students can learn to adopt and add to their repertoire of roles they can access when needed in and out of school.

A perspective is a point of view or way of seeing. A perspective provides a lens by which to see the world, much like a pair of glasses. The *TfC* method uses the concept of perspective, as point of view, to identify challenges and puzzles and to shape the research process. We utilize both the distinctive individual perspectives that students possess to see the world and disciplinary-based ethical perspectives that highlight the moral issues in the curriculum and the life of the community in the research process.

An individual perspective is formed by our circumstances, experiences, and beliefs but just as importantly, what *we do* with these circumstances and experi-ences and how we come to these beliefs. Telling someone you grew up in a family with 10 siblings conveys less than it first appears. The impact of growing up in a family of 11 children will not be same for all the members of the family. While perspectives are formed by the past, they function as a light to see the present and shape future choices and decisions.

A perspective enables a student researcher to identify problems and puzzles that others cannot or will not see. And that is just the beginning. A perspective can help a student recognize research design strategies that may exclude parts of the community, identify survey questions that are biased, and inform efforts to use knowledge gained through the research process in a way that is just, fair, and enduring.

Not surprisingly, diverse research teams often produce the best community research and are able to develop and implement action plans based on their re-search that are effective and enduring. This success is due to the fact that the team looks like the school or community it is examining. Moreover, a class with a range of perspectives is unlikely to be dominated by one particular way of see-ing and thinking. Unconscious bias creeps into and distorts the research process when everyone is seeing and thinking the same way. A single dominate perspec-tive becomes the taken-for-granted way of seeing, making it hard to even identify this lens as a bias. We are rarely aware that we are part of "group think." While a diversity of perspectives does not eliminate bias, it effectively multiplies sources of bias, thereby, making it less likely that a single bias will shape the research process.

While it is important to help students develop their individual perspectives, it is also critical for students and teachers to be self-conscious of their perspectives. Only if your students are aware of their own perspectives can they take steps to ensure that they do not pressure research subjects—even subtlety and unconsciously—to adopt to their way of seeing.

PLANNING

This step is designed to assist teachers in three planning tasks:

1. To help students develop individual attitudes and perspectives that will enable them to productively engage with the curriculum and/or their community.
2. Introduce an ethical disciplinary perspective to enrich curricular content.
3. As the first step in a semester or yearlong *TfC* research project aimed at addressing a school or community challenge or as a means of enhancing the effectiveness of an experiential, service, or civic project.

Below, we help you plan lessons and activities that can assist your students as they develop engaged proactive attitudes, surface their own perspectives, recognize the value of a classroom made up of diverse perspectives, and use ethical perspectives or ways of seeing to highlight questions about what is good, fair, or just.

Adopting an Engaged Proactive Attitude Toward the World

Engaged, proactive students have an attitude that helps them look for things that don't make sense or that seem wrong or unjust and motivates them to do something about these issues. The thinking and doing associated with this attitude have to be modeled and demonstrated in a range of ways. You can't tell students to be proactive. We have found that the two most effective techniques for helping students adopt engaged and proactive attitudes are: provide a range of examples and models of what proactive engagement looks like and/or help students recognize that they are already proactively engaging with the curriculum and the world around them every day.

Both of these approaches enable students to isolate and identify this way of engaging so that they can begin to intentionally deploy it when appropriate.

Resource

Short exercises or activities are often best for this instruction. Here is an exercise that helps students recognize and build on the proactive engagement they are already doing.

> *Teacher:* "What is your truth? What are you thinking about right now as you are sitting in this class?" Try being aware of your inner commentary. What is going through your mind right now? What are you telling yourself as you are sitting here? Whatever you are saying to yourself is evidence of engagement—even if it is a rejection of what you are hearing: "I hate this. . . . I can't believe how challenging *TfC* is."
>
> This inner voice can sometimes function as an unconscious thought—which may be felt as discomfort. Or, some of your thoughts may remind you that you need to look for more data. Other thoughts may bother or excite you so much that they give you a reason to act—"do I dare burn the calories necessary to make this class my favorite?"

The key takeaway is that *all* of these examples are the beginnings of mental engagement that students can build on.

As a teacher, you may want to have students record some of their private thoughts or share them with the class or a group. The purpose of making students aware of their inner voices is to demonstrate that engagement isn't something other people do. This is something they are already doing, and being aware of this fact makes it possible to build on their engagement, focus it, and make it do something.

Here are some comments students made to themselves and then recorded in their journals in a class that began with this activity. In addition to exhibiting individual engagement, these comments all invite a response of some kind and thus open up the possibility of groups of students engaging with one another.

> "I don't agree with that!" "Why?"
> "That is not my experience!"
> "That makes sense to me, why doesn't it make sense to others?"
> "What would you have to believe to say that?"
> "You don't conform to the stereotype I have of someone who does those things."
> "This seems like a waste, why should I bother?"
> "Our community is not going to be helped by that."
> "You keep talking about a perspective, but what is it really?"

Surfacing Distinctive Individual Perspectives

Good researchers, as novices or experienced investigators, develop their own perspectives to help them analytically engage the world. Likewise, *TfC* students learn that they all have a perspective or point of view. The question for the teacher is: Are students using their perspectives in a deliberative way? Are the questions and discussions in class providing avenues and lenses that provide young researchers with angles for seeing themselves, their family life, school, and community? When A teacher asks for students to use their perspective to help identify challenges that others might not see, the research process is already underway. Moreover, particularly at the start of the work, the research process will evolve in more creative and effective ways because of the different perspectives that individuals bring to the work.

Teachers and students need to work together to integrate the variety of perspectives that are present, but not always visible in the lab or classroom. For example, a *TfC* class realized that a community safety survey that does not take into account the fact that feeling safe or unsafe depends on the race and age of the respondent will not get good data on this question from community members. Perspectives might be more or less honest, clear, understandable, helpful, or stable, but they are never good or bad. They are never an AP, honors, or generallevel perspective. The reality students need to hear repeated in a whole range of ways is that a perspective = a way of seeing.

In *TfC*, students' perspectives can often be developed through a self-inventory. The self-inventory asks students to consider their circumstances, experiences, and beliefs as well as how they shape their way of seeing.

Resource

Here is an example of an inventory we have used to help students surface their own perspectives:

"Everyone has a story. This is mine."[1]

Ask your students to respond to the questions below and explain that you expect them to spend an engaged hour on an assignment that will get them thinking about three questions:

- What is your personal story?
- What is the perspective that you have from living this story?
- What perspective and abilities do you bring to our work?

Then, ask your students to make lists in response to the following prompt. It is not necessary for their answers to be written out in full sentences; bullets will suffice. What is important is that their answers are honest and considered.

1. Personal Inventory. Make three lists in response to the following prompts:
   a. Your most important *circumstances*—situations that you were born into and didn't choose, such as family, number of siblings, race, religion of your family—*and how they shaped you.*
   b. Your most important *life experiences*—*what lessons or skills have you learned from them.*
   c. Your most important *beliefs or values*—what you believe to be right, just, and fair—*and how they shape who you are.*
2. Now write two paragraphs that discuss the abilities and perspective you bring to our class.
   a. In the first paragraph choose a couple of abilities or skills you possess and discuss how they might contribute to the work in your classroom or in community problem solving.
   b. In the second paragraph, choose two words that describe your perspective or way of seeing and explain why you chose them and how they might be helpful for the work of inquiry in the class.

Note, that teachers have adopted this inventory to their own needs. Some have limited the self-inventory to student's circumstances and experiences. Others have included beliefs and used the ethical reasoning exercise below to help students further surface these beliefs. What is critical is to help each student be self-conscious of their perspective so that they can intentionally use it in the research process and in daily life.

ETHICAL REASONING

For most of our students, there is an ethical component to their perspective or way of seeing—what they believe to be right, just, and fair. If possible, this dimension should be acknowledged. The focus, here, is not on having the "right" beliefs or even what ethical position students take. The focus is instead on the process whereby students articulate their beliefs and clarify their values. The process by which students understand and explain how they arrive at their beliefs is called moral reasoning or moral reflection. These ethical beliefs are part of the perspective by which students see the world and can be refined through conversation with classmates, engagement with the curriculum, or through research action projects in the schools or the community. Some teachers have had their students undertake moral reflection as part of the perspective inventory described above. Other teachers have decided to use ethical reasoning to surface beliefs and values and use these as a means to identify challenges and puzzles to study. Still, other teachers, due to time constraints, have not undertaken ethical reasoning with their students and have focused on perspectives that were developed from circumstances and experiences.

Resource

Here is a lesson we have used to help students begin to understand and use moral reasoning. Introduce moral reasoning as the thinking behind beliefs and decisions regarding what is good, fair, and just and what kind of community they want to live in. Then, have your students read this Kohlberg Dilemma.[2]

> Joe[3] is 14 years old and wants to go to camp very much. His father promised him he could go if he saved up the money for it himself. So, Joe worked hard and saved up the three-hundred fifty ($350) dollars it cost to go to camp, and a little more besides. But just before camp was going to start, his father changed his mind. Some of his dad's friends decided to go on a special fishing trip, and Joe's father was short of the money it would cost. So, his father told Joe to give him the money he had saved from the paper route so he could go on the fishing trip with the other dads. Joe didn't want to give up going to camp, so he thinks of refusing to give his father the money.

To unpack the question: What is the most responsible thing for Joe to do in this situation? Ask your students to suspend judgment about whether Joe or his father's view is correct—pending a discussion that uncovers *how* they develop their answer to that question. At the conclusion of the discussion, tell your students that they will have a chance to share their recommendations for Joe and his dad as they move forward. Your preparation is to think about how you want to present this lesson given the learning objectives and purposes you are targeting and the time constraints you face. For example, if you have time, ask your students what they think the obvious question at the end of the story might be. Most often you will hear or prompt with: What should Joe do? We suggest that you then introduce a shift in thinking about that question and restate it as: What is the most responsible thing for Joe to do in this situation? Point out that the question still asks what Joe should do—however, it introduces ethical dimensions. As your students evolve in their moral reasoning, point out the connections they are making through the lens of their different perspectives. First, set the guidelines:

1. The concept of responsibility sets an expectation of what is reasonably good, fair, and just. Remind your students that reasonable behavior is determined by what most people might think, say, or do in a given situation and that there are strong legal connotations here—use juries as an example of how what is reasonable is determined through evidence and multiple perspectives.
2. The revised question speaks to being responsible in a specific situation rather than the lack of clarity suggested by "What should Joe do?" "What responsible actions should Joe take?"—narrows the question and invites inquiry with specific steps that might help find an answer, and eventually a solution.

To explore the question of what Joe can do to make a responsible decision, the following question series below may be used in a variety of ways as:

- An exercise that may be accomplished in one class discussion with recommendations as a quick ending or as homework.
- An extended inquiry with a full class discussion with related written assignments. We have found that this works well for individual students and for groups.
- The basis for debates, role plays, and as a means to discuss bias by changing the character's gender, economic factors, or the story's context and outcomes.

What does good mean?
- What does it mean to be a good son?
- What about a good father?
- Is the fact that the father promised the important thing in this situation?
- What about promises to people who we won't see again?

What does fair mean?
- Would you respond differently if you knew:
  - » That the father works hard to support the entire family?
  - » The parents just divorced?
  - » The father was seriously ill?
  - » The father often took Joe's money?
  - » The father was a model father in every way?

What would be just?
- What should be the authority of a father over his son? Does the father have a right of authority? Should he or should he not have that right?
- How do our social institutions view parental rights? Does the father have the right to tell Joe to give him the money? Does his father have a legal right to his money?
- What is the law? Are minors the owners of the money they are paid?
- Is this family fair and lawful in their dealings around money?

Ethical reflection is a recursive, lifelong process. Beliefs may shift or be tweaked over time. Ethical reasoning is best done first with students using hypothetical dilemmas (look online for dilemmas that you feel are appropriate for the age group you are working with) and then with messy classroom, school, and community challenges.

Topics and themes in the curriculum may be used as occasions for ethical reflection for testing and refining the ethical positions of our students:

1. Use of nuclear weapons
2. Torture of prisoners of war to get information

3. War on poverty
4. Progressive taxes
5. Bioethics

Similarly, research into community challenges are also occasions to practice ethical reasoning. Framing research questions and developing viable and enduring policy solutions that the community will accept regarding challenges like hunger, the right to work, and crime and punishment, help students test their own views and understand and come to terms with the views of others.

Further Applications. Have students analyze their answers and determine into which of the three most common ethical principles their beliefs fit most comfortably.

- *Welfare*, what is good is:
  - » What is best *for most people.*
  - » What ensures the health, well-being, happiness, or wealth of the *most people?*
- *Freedom*, what is just is:
  - » What ensures individual *freedom to act*—fewer laws, for example or
  - » What ensures *freedom from want* or discrimination?
- *Virtue*, is:
  - » A *particular definition* of the good.
  - » How we or our particular faith community defines a good person, a good organization, a good society.

Introducing Ethical Perspectives

Many teachers want to introduce depth to their curriculum by bringing a disciplinary-based way of seeing to their class in a single lesson or over the course of a semester. We have illustrated how moral reasoning can be used to help students surface their individual perspectives, and here we introduce the second ethical dimension of the *TfC* research method: using an ethical perspective. An ethical perspective highlights what is good, fair, or just in any context. We, and the teachers we have worked with, have found that acknowledging the moral dimension of curricular topics or community challenges increases student engagement. There are techniques and activities that can productively foster this engagement and be used with most existing curriculum, experiential, PBL, service-learning projects, and even with curriculum design.

Resources

To introduce ethical perspectives about what is right and fair in an ongoing or periodic conversation that gets your students to where you want them to go as thinkers, begin by brainstorming ways that an ethical perspective might enrich your curriculum.

Here are some prompts to begin your brainstorming process:

1. I want my students to develop their own perspective/or moral reasoning to understand the relationship between _____ and _____.
2. I want my students to understand the perspectives and influences that _____ had in relation to _____.
3. I want my students to be critical thinkers who can use _____ to better understand the human dimensions of _____.

Here Is a Second Activity. Write a statement that contains seven words or less that embodies what you most want your students to remember when they look back on what they learned in your class. Here are some that other teachers have shared:

- Fair decisions are made by diverse stakeholders.
- Justice means justice for all.
- Ethical decisions honor human dignity.
- Ethical scientific research serves the common good.
- Understanding climate change is a social responsibility.
- Economic conditions affect us all.

Bringing an Ethical Perspective to Your Classroom

The following prompts and questions have been developed to help you bring an ethical perspective to your classroom.

First, decide:

How are these learning experiences going to be structured?
- Whole class
- Groups
- Individual students

What activities work best for your students?
- Class discussion
- Debate
- Advocacy or persuasion (written or verbal)
- In-class writing
- Essay
- Mini-research assignment (web-based resource finding)
- Multimedia assignment
- Basis for class or small group brainstorm

How, where, and why will conversations about moral reasoning be most effective?

- Historic contexts
- Current issues
- Analysis of treaties, contracts, speeches, statements
- Understanding concepts such as oaths of office, codes of conduct, or ethics guidelines
- The relationship between policy and law
- As a means to understanding primary sources
- An understanding of why professional standards exist and are upheld by communities

What kinds of critical-thinking strategies do your students need to develop?

- Compare/contrast
- Parts/whole reflections
- Persuasive essay or speech
- Analysis of data, texts, or primary sources

Integrating Ethical Perspectives into the Curriculum

Open-ended questions are productive as reflective entry points to spark conversations across content areas.

What do we value in this classroom?

- What values do students in this classroom hold dear?
- What are our values in this classroom community?
- What are the values of this school or organization?

How do we retain professional integrity as researchers?

- Why is it important for researchers to be ethical?
- Why is it important to think about how one's research is derived or used?
- Why are professional standards upheld by accountable institutions? (Institutional Review Board [IRB] process, peer review, and so on)

Ethics and Community

In what ways might we find evidence of ethical values in the real world?

- What ethics do citizens expect of their government?
- What ethics do citizens expect of social institutions?
- What codes of conduct govern professions?
- What code of conduct do citizens expect of scientists?
- What kinds of situations provide examples of moral reasoning that underlie the answers to the questions above?
- To what extent should governments oversee research?

Through Lines to Stimulate Discussion. What are the roles and responsibilities of those who work for the common good of the community (government and agencies, churches, hospitals, schools, libraries, higher education, banks, and so on)?

- What is culture?
- What is moral reasoning and how do ethics apply to our lives?
- What is meant by the common good of a community?
- How is our community a system?
- What responsibilities do citizens have toward their communities?
- What kinds of ethical standards are expected of citizens in our community? How are they reinforced implicitly and explicitly?
- What ethics do citizens expect of their government and social institutions?
- What ethics are expected of researchers? Why is it important for individual researchers to be ethical?
- What is accountability and how do researchers, organizations, and governmental agencies establish and sustain and enforce accountable practices?
- Why are professional standards upheld by accountable institutions? (IRB process, peer review, and so on)

Debates That Students Care About. Moral reasoning and decision-making are the basis for understanding ethical dilemmas that have multiple dimensions depending on the circumstances and experiences of a group of stakeholders. After using the activities that we suggest in this step to uncover individual perspectives, it may be useful to teach civil discourse through the use of debate.

Encouraging debate can be a way of encouraging civil discourse, which includes learning to respect others through the use of manners, protocols, rules, and communication styles. The purpose is to have all arguments aired, challenged, and heard. Ethical dilemmas stir emotions as students get in touch with the powerful force of their values and perspectives. While the "I am" statements are reflective, a debate shows the power of cultural influence in action. Debates have a structure that contains this emotional force and encourages thought—thinking on one's feet, so to speak. Responses in a debate are supported by evidence—similarly to all research arguments. Debate encourages students to develop and support their ideas and practice behaviors that need to be cultivated in order to engage in discussions around important issues in the adult world.

Teachers have the opportunity in a debate to not only understand how their students think and formulate ideas, but, in a larger gestalt, to use arguments that are raised as data so that after a debate students can revisit differing views and clearly see how "I am" drives a healthy discourse.

Ethics as a basis for debate helps students to:

- Evaluate differing opinions and compare them to their own.
- Use critical thought as a prelude to decision-making.
- Help inoculate students against following the crowd before considering alternative options.

TEACHING

Over the years, we and the teachers we have been lucky to work with have developed a cluster of insights that can help teachers assist students in developing their own engaged perspectives and/or utilize ethical perspectives in their learning.

First, in as much as possible, engage in the work yourself. Being proactive, surfacing perspectives, doing ethical reasoning, and acknowledging issues of justice and fairness are lifelong, never to be completed, adult activities. *TfC* is animated by the conviction that if presented correctly, students are ready to begin this serious work. Bill and Valerie surface their perspectives with each class because it sharpens their teaching and research. They are open—in a manner that does not cut off student learning—about the fact that they too grapple with ethical questions in their lives because those dilemmas inform decisions about what is right, fair, and just as thinkers, parents, adult children, authors, voters, and educators.

Second, developing a perspective and engaging with ethical questions is work that is necessarily recursive. Let your students know that perspectives evolve through experience, and introduce the idea of satisfaction with incomplete understandings. Know that you are giving your students a powerful tool that will help them each time they both encounter the concept of a perspective and employ their own perspective to understand themselves and see the world.

Third, remind students to connect who they are and what they see to research. We use lots of examples of researchers whose work comes directly or indirectly from their lives. The best teachers often link what they find interesting to who they are, what they have done, and where they have been. For example, Bill and Valerie are both interested in issues of segregation. However, they come from different perspectives:

> *Bill:* "I got interested in segregation because my first job was teaching in Baltimore City Public Schools."
> *Valerie:* "I got interested in segregation because I was born in Apartheid South Africa."

Finally, while it is tempting to focus on the moral judgments student make, for example, about gun control, try to emphasize the *process* by which students arrive at moral judgments. *TfC* is focused on inquiry—*not* self-expression, analyzing motives, or being right. We find that the simplest way to guide students toward the exercise of moral reasoning is to ask:

- Why do you believe that?
- What evidence do you have to support your belief or judgment?
- Now that you can explain to yourself why you believe what you do, do you want to revise your judgment? Why or why not?

ASSESSMENT

Formative Assessment

Self-Assessment: Survey. After completing the *My Story* exercise above, have students answer the six questions below, which are designed to both help them assess what they have learned from surfacing their own perspective and begin thinking about empirical research.

1. I did not spend an engaged hour on this assignment because I was:
   a. Distracted
   b. Not interested enough
   c. None of the above _____
2. I fully engaged with the assignment.
   a. True
   b. False
   c. Not sure what engaged means
3. What would you point to in your assignment that would convince someone of your engagement? _____
4. What was the hardest part of this assignment?
   a. Doing the personal inventory
   b. Fighting the urge to find the RIGHT answer
   c. Deciding what I can offer the class
   d. Choosing two words to describe my perspective
5. Recommend one change that would improve this assignment for future students. _____
6. If you had to give this survey a grade for how well it assessed your experience with the *"Everyone has a story, this is mine"* assignment, what would you give it?
   a. Excellent
   b. Good
   c. Failing

Rubrics. These may be administered at the start of work or retrospectively—with students identifying their strengths and weaknesses, setting and assessing learning targets, and evaluating outcomes. The identification of student's strengths and weaknesses may provide a starting point for each student to set their own behavioral and participation goals and/or as a follow-up self-assessment at the conclusion of work. For semester or yearlong research projects, have students take the *Self-Assessment Rubric*—of course, pick the elements in the rubric that fit your needs (Appendix A)—and/or the *Seeing and Being Rubric* (Appendix B) as a diagnostic aid to identify strengths and weaknesses prior to beginning *TfC*.

Teacher Observation: Group Discussion. The exercise *My Story* might be a component of a two-part oral and written assignment that is used as a formative assessment. Students should be told in advance that they are in an assessed discussion and be informed about the criteria and scope of what is expected. We generally have students break into groups to brainstorm inventories of experience and circumstances and, then, have students complete the written portion of this assignment independently.

Observational criteria:
- Are students actively listening to one another?
- Are students asking constructive questions of one another in order to support one another as they inventory experiences or are individuals' behaviors inhibiting this work?

Outcomes that might be immediately evident:
- In what specific ways have students demonstrated an expanded understanding of one another's lives through sharing their circumstances and experiences? (Example: Pair shares in which students tell each other's stories and reflect on possible meanings.)
- What do students observe about changes in classroom climate that would not have occurred had they not had the opportunity to learn about each other's lives?

Research Journal Entries:
1. Choose one question to respond to in two sentences:
    » Do you think there are different styles of engagement based on race?
    » Do you think there are different styles of engagement based on income?
    » Do you think there are different styles of engagement based on gender?
2. Describe someone you know who is engaged in their life in ways that demonstrate commitment, tenacity, and a positive attitude.

Summative Assessment

Individual Performance Task. After completing the exercise, *My Story*, have students interview their parent or guardian using the following questions and record. (Be sure to have each student explain to their parent/guardian how they are using the terms "circumstances" and "experiences.")

Interview questions:
- What are the key circumstances of your life and how have they shaped you?
- What are the key experiences in your life and what you learned from them?
- With your circumstances and experiences in mind: What perspective do you bring to life?

Making Curricular Connections

Perspective is a critical concept in fiction as well as nonfiction writing. For example, what distinguishes the past (*all* that has occurred) from history (one path through the past)? It is the historian's perspective or way of seeing. A perspective allows the historian to decide what is critical, indeed, what is history. Like the perspective a *TfC* student develops, historical perspectives are numerous and they are informed by context and experience.

Discuss with a fellow student or a field expert the following prompt:

Which historical perspectives would be most helpful in understanding:
- The creation of the U.S. Constitution (farmers, merchants, slaves, and so on).
- The fall of the Roman Empire?
- The coming of the French Revolution?
- The Civil Rights Movement?

FREQUENTLY ASKED QUESTIONS

Q. Why do you emphasize surfacing a perspective and not identity?

A. Surfacing an individual perspective is a way to directly channel what is distinctive within our students in a manner that is forward looking and directly contributes to the research process, which is the focus of *TfC*. Reflection and discussion of identity is, of course, helpful in a range of activities, but it does not necessarily prepare students to participate in collaborative research.

Q. How can we help students move from generating a list of their experiences, circumstances, and beliefs to a way of seeing that can contribute to inquiry?

A. This is a two-step process. The first step involves asking students how the circumstances they have listed have *shaped* them or what they have *learned* from certain experiences they have had. This way, students are making circumstances and experiences their own; not things that happen to them and that they passively receive. Being white or an only child does not mean the same thing to everyone who is white or an only child. Realizing that circumstances can be received and used in many ways also makes it easier for students to make the jump from who they are and how they see to what they can bring to inquiry.

    The second step is to ask students directly to speak or write about what—given their perspective—they can contribute to addressing classroom or community challenges. Here is what that might look like: One *TfC* student wrote that "being from a one-parent family enabled her to make sure we ask survey questions that don't assume everyone has two parents."

Q. How do you protect confidentiality when students are documenting very private life circumstances?

A. We emphasize in many different ways that the purpose of developing a perspective is to understand how one sees the world, what one is drawn to, what catches one's eye, what sensitivities one has, what you can do, NOT to discuss your personal life. We understand these are not hard and fast categories. Indeed, the challenge here is one of emphasis and ultimate purpose. We model and provide examples of individual inventories that are focused on what we see. Finally, we do not ask the students to share their perspectives or the work they have undertaken to surface them (although many wish to do so), but rather we encourage students to simply demonstrate in the course of the project of class work that they are enriching the research work with their own way of seeing. In any instance in which a student might divulge personal information that requires adult intervention, teachers should speak to the student and enlist the assistance of administrators, school counselors, psychologists, and social workers.

Q. Isn't there a danger that when students are encouraged to use their own perspectives in the inquiry process that they will be unable to be open to the perspectives of others they might encounter in their classroom or in the community?

A. We are convinced that students can understand that who they are will impact what they see and what they can contribute to the class *and* recognize that research is about making sense of the actions and beliefs of others. Students can also come to understand that they can't do the latter if they are convinced that they have the "right way" of acting and the correct beliefs. This is why being aware of personal perspectives is so important for researchers. Sure, a perspective draws us to certain questions; however, it is impossible to bound or bracket our own beliefs and let historical figures and—for example—the participants in our focus group, speak if we are not aware of our own perspective. This is also why the ethical dimension of *TfC* is focused on explaining *why* we hold the beliefs we do and understanding why others hold the beliefs they do, not on simply advancing beliefs—for example—about whether the death penalty is right and wrong.

eTOOLBOX: RESOURCES

A range of resources for this step—including, hints, activities, lecture outlines, and samples of student work—may be found on the resource page of the *TfC* website: https://www.tools4changeseminar.com/resources.html

Question
Identifying and Framing Empirical Research Questions

There is simply not enough time to investigate every aspect of an issue of interest in the curriculum or the community. A research question provides the focus necessary to start the research process and bring it to completion. That is why the first question one researcher asks another is: "What is your question?" Identifying what students care about and translating this interest into research questions that can be answered with new data is the focus of this step and the focal point of the *TfC* research method. Learning to frame empirical research questions is best done by following pathways that the community of researchers have worked out through years of experience and then having your students practice on their own. In Step 2, we provide entry points to these pathways and then provide exercises that help students frame their own productive research questions.

CASE STUDY

We have found that students have difficulty using their newly developed perspectives to simply brainstorm topics or ideas they want to explore. When something concrete is introduced that students can engage with and push off against, it is sometimes easier for them to see the best ways to leverage their perspectives. In the early stages of a *TfC* class, Valerie invited two government officials to speak about the biggest challenges facing their town. Two experienced *TfC* students conducted the interview, modeling the respect and focus that all good interviews have. (In other classes, teachers have conducted and modeled good interview techniques at this step in the research process.) The other students in the class took notes and later asked questions to clarify what they had heard. During the conversation, one official mentioned that the town had started an initiative to address hunger in the community by, first, making a comprehensive list of the organizations that were working on the issue and, then, starting to interview the leaders of these organizations.

After the presentation, the students in the class expressed a strong interest in the topic of hunger. Valerie thought this was a good idea because hunger is an issue that young people can relate to, regardless of their backgrounds. Additionally, if the class focused on hunger, classroom research could be aligned with the ongoing work by the town. The possibility of coproducing a hunger initiative with the town was very attractive to the students. So far, so good.

Subsequent class discussions quickly revealed that while community hunger was a topic of interest, there was very little agreement on what aspect of this topic the class should focus on. Several possible research questions that would provide this focus were advanced. In deciding among these possible questions, students found it difficult to see the connection between a research question and what would be involved in actually answering that question. They grappled with how long it would take, what work was involved, and what it would look like to actually do it.

Framing Empirical Research Questions for School and Community Research Projects

Valerie decided that the teacher curation work in this step should center on helping the students see the research implications of the questions they developed. Then—she thought—armed with this knowledge, students could decide which question they wanted to try to answer.

Resource

Here is how the class worked through the implications of one of the research questions they brainstormed.

Proposed research question: *How do hunger-related organizations work together to address hunger in our community?*

Who are the community leaders and research subjects who could provide data to answer our question?
- Who are the community leaders on the list that the town is putting together?
- How might we identify leaders of organizations that work on hunger in the county—soup kitchens, community pantries, and advocacy groups?
- Who are the people these organizations serve?

What data collection methods might we use?
- Should we use surveys only?
- Should we use focus groups only?
- Should we use both surveys and focus groups?

How will our research have an impact?
- Are we identifying gaps that no one is presently focusing on?
- Is our purpose to publicize to people who need hunger-related help what services are available and where?

- Is our purpose to help organizations develop more effective ways to work with each other?

What are the challenges?
- Do we have the time and bandwidth to contact all the organizations involved?
- Can we convince them to take a survey or arrange a time for a focus group?

After a vigorous debate grounded in the specifics of the possible research, the class decided to move forward with this research question.

In the course of the research, Valerie and her students refined the question several times. Three months later, after a series of focus groups (carefully designed to complement the interviews that the town was conducting) with leaders of community kitchens and food pantries, the students found that the organizations' leaders were not communicating with each other and were in fact actively competing for grants and food donations from businesses in the area. The project culminated with the class co-convening a monthly leadership meeting designed to make it easy for the representatives of food pantries and community kitchens to exchange information that would lower incidences of food waste that might otherwise have fed the hungry.

KEY FEATURES

Most social science research, and the *TfC* method in particular, begins with the identification of an issue that is more interesting and alluring than manageable. The challenge, then, is to translate that issue into a research question that retains what is of interest *and* can be answered under existing constraints.

The ability to see what is strange, confusing, or unjust as opportunities to understand and explain, on the one hand, and the discipline necessary to define the issue so that it can be grasped and analyzed, on the other, are two different, but related, skills and dispositions. It is easier to see this in action. Thankfully, there is no shortage of examples of what is intriguing, complex, or meaningful. Issues worth our time to investigate are all around us if we only look. For example, we present an excerpt from an interview with Sendhi Mullainatahn, computational and behavioral scientist and a MacArthur Genius Award winner.[1] To be sure Mullainatahn has more practice at "exploring" the world for what is interesting and then translating what is interesting into a research project than most of us, but we can all learn from how he does this.

Question: I was looking into your work, you have done research on all kinds of things, hedge fund profits, racial discrimination, cigarette tax, energy policies, and government corruption and . . . I could do this for a while. What is the through line in your work?

Answer: I just love, love, love, love thinking and I love exploring. So, I am never going to, you know, climb Mount Everest. . . . I am not that kind of adventurous person and most of those places are also already explored. But in the intellectual space the ability to go to a whole new place, a place no one has ever been . . . this is just so exciting. I also love dessert. I love biting into an amazing chocolate chip cookie. But when you have a new idea, it is even more pleasurable. I don't mean intellectually pleasurable. [I mean pleasurable] at primitive level.

For me, I end up wandering from areas because I enjoy being in new spaces where no one is, like being in the wilderness.

Question: How do you decide when you have something to bring to a topic?

Answer: What I look for are blind spots [in how we understand a problem]. For example, the way we tax cigarettes [at a very high rate] . . . . There was a whole discussion [on this] very well thought out [that focused on] what does it do to [rates] of smoking. There was a blind spot here: what is the experience of being a smoker? Psychologists tell us that some people like it [smoking]. That is fine. But some people are struggling to quit. So, I put myself in the shoes of that person, how would they feel about a cigarette tax, I would be annoyed, now this thing costs more. But maybe I would be kind of happy, then I would say maybe this might help me quit. Maybe not in the moment, but maybe a few months later I would be happy. Then we went to "quit lines" [call in services to help people quit smoking] and found that when the tax goes up there is a spike in calls coming into quit lines. Maybe antidotal, but intriguing a relative blind spot. . . . Wouldn't it be funny if they became happier if they were taxed? So, that starts the journey. So, this is how I work, find a new thing, I try to find a blind spot.

We hope that you and your students think of beginning research like biting into a great chocolate chip cookie—as pleasurable, as something they want to do. Like Mullainatahn, you and your students can often find topics to study by trying to see life from someone else's perspective.

Turning an interesting observation into an empirical question that can be answered with data is a discipline. It is a discipline because there is a right and a wrong way to construct a research question that follows a well-tested technique. To take Mullainatahn's conjecture about smokers and taxes as an example, we can't know if taxes make smokers happy unless we narrow our focus. Framing a research question—for example, what is the relationship between the happiness of a smoker and a tax on cigarettes?—is the way researchers tell themselves, other researchers, and the public what they are focusing on.

PLANNING

This step is designed to help teachers and students frame research questions for both:

1. Short curricular enrichment lessons or exercises.
2. As part of a semester or yearlong *TfC* research project or as a means to bring analytical focus to a C3 Inquiry, a PBL, or an experiential, service, or civic project.

Planning in this step begins by helping students develop the ability to seek out and identify what doesn't make sense, seems unfair, or appears unjust in the curriculum. Then students learn to turn these issues and topics, puzzles and problems into research questions that can be answered. School or community challenges can be similarly framed as larger empirical questions that may animate a semester elective or a yearlong PBL program, service, or action-research project.

Identifying Puzzles and Problems

For short curricular excursions, many teachers identify the problem or puzzle. When students are asked to take the lead, we have found that even if they have surfaced an engaged perspective (Step 1), they often find that identifying an issue that is either strange or interesting—*and* that they care about—is very difficult and even paralyzing. Often when students do identify an issue of concern, they frequently approach the issue in tired or predictable ways that overlook what they—and they alone as young people—can bring to the topic. It is often useful to give students materials that either illustrate how what doesn't make sense can be a point of departure for inquiry or simply serve as something to push off against and get ideas. Teachers have—like Valerie in the case study— invited experts or community leaders into the class, provided prompts based on student discussions, and then used local newspapers and census data to explore these prompts. Or, alternatively, they have had students read articles that highlight issues they have talked about or that high school students might have a special interest in—such as why 16-year-olds were allowed to vote in the referendum that decided whether Scotland would remain in the United Kingdom in 2015.

Students typically have a lot to say when they are asked this question: "What doesn't make sense in the world?" There are huge parts of their lives that don't make sense to them. From the simplest situation, such as coming into a room full of people and asking what is going on, to the increasing presence of global health issues, terrorism, and violence, students can easily identify which parts of the adult world most challenge their common sense. What seems funny or hypocritical even though it isn't supposed to be? Getting into the habit of seeing what doesn't fit or seems odd is a good way to identify issues of interest.

Resource

Here is an exercise that gives students practice identifying what doesn't make sense as a first step in surfacing issues they care about.

Background. We have provided the first paragraph of an article on the Ford Foundation. The Ford Foundation gives money to groups and organizations who want to make the world better. From long experience funding projects, the foundation has learned all the ways efforts to make the world a better place *fail*. The paragraph lists these reasons. We share this paragraph with students (and help with vocabulary they may not understand) as an example of a puzzle that doesn't make sense. Here, the list contains a number of items, some of which seem odd and surprising.

Activity. We ask students to read this paragraph:

The urge to change the world is normally thwarted by a near insurmountable barricade of obstacles: failure of imagination, failure of courage, bad government, bad planning, incompetence, corruption, fecklessness, the laws of nations, the laws of physics, the weight of history, inertia of all sorts, psychological unsuitability on the part of would be changers, the resistance of people who would lose for the change, the resistance of people who would benefit from it, the seduction of activities other than world changing, lack of practical knowledge, lack of political skill, lack of money.[2]

Then, we ask students to:

- Pick the items on this list of reasons why well-intentioned projects *don't* work that are most surprising to you—for example, many students are surprised that a project might fail because of "resistance from people who would benefit from it." (We have also asked students to identify items on the list that don't seem to make sense—for example, "the laws of physics"—and have students try to develop explanations for why they belong on the list.)
- Try to give a one-sentence explanation for why the author of this paragraph might nevertheless have included this "surprising" reason why change doesn't happen.
- Pick one of the "surprising" reasons and discuss what would have to be done to remove this obstacle to positive change.

Moving from What Is Interesting to a Research Question

The thinking and doing required to move from what is interesting to a research question can be taught in a lesson or series of lessons. Framing an effective research

question is also an indispensable first step in a semester or yearlong research project (such as in AP Capstone) or addressing a school or community problem.

The process of turning what is interesting into a question that can be answered with new evidence has two dimensions.

1. *Tradeoffs.* Making hard choices about what is possible and doable in regard
   to the research.
2. *Techniques.* Honing the skills necessary to write effective questions.

When researchers translate an interesting topic into a research question, they
are narrowing and limiting their focus. They are trading breadth for precision.
No one likes to give things up. This narrowing, however, is necessary to make
an issue manageable so students can experience the research process in the time
available. There is no right way to narrow one's focus. Instead, the goal is to be
aware of the trade-offs: what you are giving up and what you are getting when
you narrow or refine a question.

Resource

Here is an example of how a *TfC* team explained why they chose their research
question:

> We chose the question—"What is the relationship between a person's family
> size and their willingness to get food stamps?"—after reading many of the
> personal stories written about people who are hungry. Many of the stories
> that we read were about individuals who had many young children who
> needed to be fed. It is difficult to acknowledge that you need food stamps.
> However, when your children are also facing hunger, it's even more difficult
> to ignore your hungry children. It seems as though many individuals,
> especially mothers, are getting food stamps in order to feed children. This
> relationship definitely caught our attention. We think that as a whole any
> relationships that include a 'person's willingness to get food stamps' is
> definitely something we should focus on.[3]

Effective Research Questions. Not all questions are productive empirical
research questions—that is, a question that can be answered with new data.
Research questions have patterns that distinguish them from other kinds of questions. Framing effective research questions is about understanding these patterns and practicing writing questions that fit these patterns. Students (and even
teachers) need to be reminded that there are three broad categories of questions.

The first two types are ***not*** research questions. The question types are:

- Questions that can be answered by a fact.
  Example: What year was Malcolm X born? How did the Korean War start?

- Questions that require opinions and speculation to answer.
  Example: Do you support the death penalty?

Effective empirical research questions ask:

- Why something happens.
  Example: Why do people so often blame themselves when they
    lose their job?
- If a relationship exists and what the true nature of that
  relationship is.
  Example: What is the relationship between worrying about money
    and a lack of motivation to work?
- Whether a hypothesis about how something happens or how two
  things are related is correct.
  Example: Does the anxiety associated with poverty make it harder
    for children to focus in school?

Resource

Here are some examples that illustrate the relationship between an issue of interest and a research question:

Issue: Young people are concerned about living in a high crime area.
- A possible research question: Are young people more likely to be
  victims of crime? How would you find out?

Issue: A diverse community is trying to increase civic engagement.
- *A possible research question:* How does race influence community
  involvement? How would you find out?

Issue: In an effort to encourage teens to become more involved in their
community, a high school has introduced a new civics program.
- *A possible research question:* What impact does a high school civics class
  have on the community involvement of students who take the class?
  How would you find out?

Issue: Citizens in an economically disadvantaged community report that
the local police are not helpful and people in a middle-class neighborhood
report that the police are helpful.
- *A possible research question:* Does income impact people's perceptions of
  the police? How would you find out?

Issue: The number of people voting in local elections in a town has declined
dramatically in the last four elections.
- *A possible research question:* What factors influence people to vote in the
  town? How would you find out?

Resource: Checklist for Effective *TfC* Research Questions:

1. Is the question:
    - *relevant* to the curriculum, current events, school improvement plans?
    - *of genuine interest* to your students?
    - *reflective* of students' perspectives?
2. Does the question have an *ethical* dimension that challenges students and community members?
    - Does it enable students and community members to inquire and reflect on what is good, fair, right, or just?
    - Many research questions have an ethical dimension. Here are the six research and teaching areas in the Kenan Institute for Ethics at Duke University:
        a. Environmental Policy
        b. Global Migration
        c. Regulation
        d. Human Rights
        e. Moral Attitudes and Decision Making
        f. Religion and Public Life
3. Can the question be answered with *new data* that can be collected by students in the time available and within constraints that exist?
4. Can *other researchers or community members* interested in your question make use of the findings that might emerge from this question?

Resource: A Practice Template to Jumpstart the Practice of Crafting Research Questions

Try inserting words into these sentence templates so that they make sense for your topic:

1. What is the relationship between _____ and _____?
2. How do relationships between _____ and _____ influence _____?
3. How does _____ influence _____ and _____?
4. To what extent does the relationship between _____ and _____ impact _____?
5. What are the perceptions of (group of people) _____ to _____?

Time and Choices for Semester or Yearlong Research Projects

The way you frame the research question will shape the subsequent steps in the research process. One teacher put the curating challenge of framing research questions for empirical research projects in the following terms: How do we honor the interests and commitments of our students *and* frame questions that are ethical and doable in the time we have?

There is no "right" way to teach your students how to frame a research question that will both engage them for a semester or a year *and* is doable under the constraints you are working under. Which strategy you choose depends on your needs and circumstances, the amount of time you have, and the role you want your students to play in determining the research question.

TfC teachers have employed three basic strategies to develop a research question for their class:

1. *Choose* the question they want their students to focus on—such as a pressing issue in the community that fits with a unit in the English language arts or social studies curriculum.
2. *Present* students with a curated set of topics to convert into research questions and then ask students to develop presentations that make a case for one of these topics. The class can vote on the one they want to focus on.
3. *Offer* the choice of possible topics and the content of the final research question wholly up to their students.

After more than a decade of working with students and teachers, we strongly recommend that you over, rather than under, curate this step—that is, do not leave the choice entirely up to your students except under unique circumstances. Most teachers have found that reaching consensus on a topic is extremely difficult and very time-consuming. Students can sometimes become disengaged from the research process if they have been told they can choose the research topic and the class does not select "their" topic.

Good relationships make it possible to be honest with our students as we facilitate the research experience. Students sometimes make suggestions for research topics that are inappropriate at school and it is our job to explain why. We are open with our students as we explain confidentiality issues around the release of student information, why we can't ask whether a student is eligible for free or reduced lunch, that medical information is protected, or that adults won't want to discuss certain issues with young people. For example, students may be interested in why homelessness exists in their community and you may be aware that a student is or was homeless. To protect student privacy and ensure that no one is uncomfortable, it is best to suggest an alternative focus. Here, a redirect toward organizations that address hunger in the community or contact with social workers who work with homeless young people might allow students to retain what they care about in a topic and provide a respectful way to approach that topic. In another example, when students shared that they wanted to lower the voting age in national elections to 16 years of age, we needed to be able to help them "shrink" the topic so what was originally interesting could be explored in the time available. In this example, we narrowed the issue rather than abandoning it by suggesting that our students focus on lowering the voting age in school board elections in their district, a much more manageable option for everyone.

TEACHING

Over the years we, and the teachers with whom we have worked, have developed a cluster of insights that can help you assist your students in framing research questions.

First, make it personal. Often the most effective way to help students identify issues of concern is for you to simply be honest in a matter-of-fact manner about what doesn't make sense, what seems odd, strange, or wrong in your life, and what you do to try to figure out some of these puzzles. Indeed, even how you decide which among the hundreds of puzzles in your life you will try to understand and explain—is there a pattern to the puzzles you attend to and the ones you ignore?—would be helpful for students to hear.

Second, remind students to use their perspectives. Being self-conscious about how they see the world and how to use what their perspective highlights is a new habit that requires practice. Pair students who have special gifts, skills, and sensibilities—especially nonacademic ones—with students who wish to develop these skills.

Third, and finally, determining where and how student autonomy and freedom should be augmented by your own curation of the research process is or should be an ongoing task. You should recalibrate with your class and individual students as time goes on and try to embrace the open-ended nature of this work.

ASSESSMENT

Formative

Research Journal Entries:
- Ask students to share an example in their life in which they asked the wrong question.
- Ask students to reflect (orally or in writing) on how the perspectives in the class are or are not evident in the research question that has been selected.

Summative

Curate materials (census data, local newspapers, and/or health, crime, or quality of life data) for students to examine and have them answer the following questions:

- List and discuss two things you learned that most surprised you about your town/community/city.
- List and discuss the most important challenges confronting your community that are illustrated in these materials and then discuss whether you can see yourself in these problems, or have felt or seen the consequences of these problems, or are willing to explore ways that you can understand the consequences of these challenges in the future.
- Choose an issue you think your class should examine this year and develop a research question and a one paragraph argument for why this question is important and why your class should address it.
- Develop interview questions and then interview a city official or community leader about what they see as the most pressing challenges in the community.

Making Curricular Connections

ELA Connections. Ask students to edit a draft introduction of a research report written by another *TfC* research team (examples can be found in the Resources page of the *TfC* website). This editing work should include suggestions that will ensure the introduction does what it is intended to do as well as basic grammar and style. Does the introduction:

1. Clearly state the research question?
2. Give the reader the information they need to understand the research question?
3. Make the reader want to read the rest of the report?

Civics Connections. Civics classes often focus on specific ways students can serve their communities and participate responsibly in civil society and the political process. Ask your students to make the case that the analytical and ethical work they are doing in their *TfC* class is an example of community service.

We have found students enjoy civic participation that is analytical. For example, a group of students in Valerie's high school surveyed public attitudes toward water quality in their community to counter a negative media campaign by a water filter company that had shaken public confidence.

FREQUENTLY ASKED QUESTIONS

Q. What can a teacher do if they are not happy with the question their class selects for an enrichment activity?

A. If at all possible, try to treat teaching *TfC* as itself as a research experiment. Because you are not covering content but learning a skill, it should be possible to learn how to do research from our successes as well as our failures. We can certainly learn a lot from imperfect research questions. First, record what the challenges were in framing a question so that this knowledge can inform future practice—how did you curate the process, where did students go off track? Then, try to ensure you and your students learn as much as they can from trying to answer the imperfect question. For example, the answers a group of students received when they interviewed parents about their knowledge of impeachment were not on point because they mentioned President Clinton in the question and only got opinions on his presidency. Lesson: Make sure your research question doesn't distract respondents from the main issue. In some cases, you can apply what you and your students learn right away, by revising or tweaking the question based on preliminary research. In other cases, the learning may take the form of making it clear to students that the problems they encountered were directly related to the way they asked the question.

eTOOLBOX: RESOURCES

A range of resources for this step—including, hints, activities, lecture outlines, and samples of student work—may be found on the resource page of the *TfC* website: https://www.tools4changeseminar.com/resources.html

Conversation

"Conversing" with Other Researchers and Writing a Literature Review

Social science research is a people activity. The questions that interest social scientists involve people and how they interact. Research builds on the work of previous researchers. Findings and policy recommendations are helpful to the extent that people can test, implement, and build on them. We tell our students that researchers are part of a big club, whose members come from every country in the world and who believe problems are best solved with evidence, not opinions and feelings. This club is made up of other researchers, government officials, leaders of NGOs, community leaders, and policy-makers at all levels. We think that high school students should start acting as if they too are members of this club.

It is simply smart for students to take advantage of the knowledge and wisdom of other members of this club before they embark on their own work, whether it is producing a research paper or a literature review for a PBL project or a semester or yearlong *TfC* community problem-solving research project. The ability of your students to respectfully "converse" with sources makes it possible to realize the benefits of previous wisdom and experience. This *TfC* step shows you and your students how to have these conversations.

CASE STUDY

The case study that follows illustrates how one teacher helped her students curate a conversation with sources. Sarah, a new teacher in rural eastern North Carolina, was devoting class time from her U.S. history class so her students could work on a community research project. Together, she and her students identified an issue they cared about—community safety—and then framed a research question: What is the relationship between leisure, poverty, and violence in Halifax and Northampton Counties, North Carolina?

Her first thought as she began planning the research project was: *Do Americans have a right to safety in their communities that the government has an obligation to protect?* This initial thought was reflected in the way she planned the literature review for the class. Sarah knew that many of the students had little confidence that anything would change in their community—for example, that county leaders would address the issue of violence by investing in safe alternatives. She suggested that one section of the class literature review might be titled "A Right to Community Safety." Then, she planned a class in which her students would have a conversation with the Bill of Rights, which they had been reading in class to see if it promised this right to safety.

She began the class by saying:

It just makes sense to learn what other qualified people have to teach us about the question we are trying to answer. If you wanted to learn a new dance routine, you would actively seek out YouTube videos and other Internet resources and learn what is out there. The video says, "Here is how you do this part of the dance," and you ask, "How much do you have to bend your knees to do that?" It is easy to imagine having a conversation with a person or even talking back to a YouTube video. Now, I want to convince you today that you can converse or speak with a piece of paper written hundreds of years ago—that is, have a give and take conversation with the "Founding Fathers" of our nation. Today, I want to show you how you can have a conversation with the first 10 amendments of the Bill of Rights to see if they can help us answer our research question. Why the Bill of Rights? Because I want to know if all Americans have a right to safety in their communities. The Bill of Rights is the first place to look to see if this right exists. And, if there is a right to safety then we are not asking for something special, we are just asking for what is ours under the highest law in the land, the Constitution.

Then, she asked two of her students to take notes so the substance of this conversation could be later shaped and expanded when the class wrote the literature review section of the report they were planning. Then, she worked through the first 10 amendments with the class, asking them to select the ones that were most likely to answer the question about a right to safety in one's community. Several students pointed to the Second Amendment, which says, "A well-regulated Militia, being necessary to the security of a Free State, the right of the people to keep and bear Arms, shall not be infringed."

Sarah began the conversation with the Second Amendment by noting that, "When the Second Amendment is spoken about today, it is mostly to understand if we have a right to possess guns, but that is not the only question you can you can ask this amendment. We want to ask about safety in the community."

"So, my first thought," she continued, "is how interesting. Americans have a right to keep weapons. Given our interest I would like to know: Why would people want or need a right to keep weapons? Are they worried that a foreign army might invade and everyone would need to defend America—this, after all, was the situation during the Revolutionary War. Or, were the writers thinking that people needed weapons to keep themselves safe in their communities—to protect themselves from bad neighbors. If yes, this would suggest that the writers of the Bill or Rights thought that one way to keep communities safe was to give people the right to keep weapons."

The students were asked to answer these questions by looking at the Second Amendment. The first thing that caught their eyes was the word "militia." What is the purpose of a militia, one asked? Another wanted to know if militias are set up to fight wars or are they like a police force? One student volunteered to look on Wikipedia and found that it said that a militia is "a military force." This was evidence that the Founding Fathers may not have been primarily talking about community safety when they advanced the right to bear arms.

Here's how student note takers recorded the conversation:

1. What we know from this conversation:
   * The Second Amendment doesn't speak directly about community safety.
   * It does talk about the right to bear arms.
   * This right is related to what militias do, which seems to be military in nature.
2. What would we like to know, if we have time?
   * Did militias keep communities safe?
3. How does this help us answer our research question?
   * The Second Amendment doesn't give a right to safety in our communities; it speaks about the right to own guns.
   * We are not sure if this right to keep guns is related to community safety, but we do know that there is a military reason for the right to keep guns.

In subsequent classes, students had their own *conversation* with the North Carolina Constitution to see if there was a state right to safety in the community, used the notes that were recorded as a basis for the literature review section of their report, and then developed and administered a survey asking people in the community when and where they felt safe. One of the key findings from their survey was that residents felt that county parks—intended to provide leisure for people—were among the most dangerous areas in their communities.

We recognize that these kinds of conversations are occurring in many classrooms across the country. And your conversation about the Second Amendment might be different than the one Sarah had with her class. What we want to highlight here is the fact that what makes this conversation good pedagogy is also what makes it a sound inquiry skill, a skill that should be explicitly identified for students and deliberately cultivated.

KEY FEATURES

You and your students can't answer open-ended questions that emerge from the curriculum or from community concerns by simply receiving and retrieving information. In content curriculum, students need to interrogate and shape the information they encounter. In community research projects, students must enlist existing research and/or wise experts to help them answer their questions. In either case, the process must go beyond giving students information, no matter how interesting.

The phrase "literature review" is not often used in middle or high school. When the phrase is used, it is frequently associated with answering essential questions with documents (DBQs). This usually involves pulling relevant information from a curated group of articles in order to answer a comparison/contrast question that has a correct answer. These assignments can range from short paragraph answers to five-page research papers. Increasingly, the end product is presented in a range of creative ways, including video. Students learn much that is useful from DBQs, beginning with the ability to identify relevant information.

The *TfC* method highlights the phrase "literature review" in an effort to help teachers give their students a different kind of stretch, one that is more aligned with college and career. This stretch is focused on answering open-ended questions that do not have a right answer and are not "drillable." Answering these questions requires that a student *converse* with sources and not simply identify, move, and organize information within these sources. Researchers around the world call knowledge exchanges, encounters, and conversations, a literature review. This is a term of art that students will see in college and in many professions and thus it is worth using consistently with your students.

The words "literature" and "review" point to the new place you and your students are going. "Literature" means works of value or usefulness. In *TfC* research, useful works include: newspaper and journal articles, reports, official documents, and statistics, as well as valuable insights from wise and experienced people who possess knowledge relevant to your question. The word "review" reminds us that researchers need to evaluate and analyze—that is, *question*—relevant sources to ensure that they are helpful for our specific work. What distinguishes reviewing from copying (or downloading) is the proactive engagement that is required.

PLANNING

Having a conversation with other researchers and recording the results of this conversation isn't like applying for a driver's license or a passport, where a single error will send you to the back of the line. It is more like speaking with a small group of people who are as interested as you and your students are in the subject. Exposing your students to examples of how others have conversed with sources and gaining the confidence to do this themselves is what is emphasized in this planning section.

The point of the conversation is the process, the give and take, not the conclusion. Students get better at conversations with other researchers by being aware of the question they are coming to the conversation with and trying to be open to all the different ways the conversation can help them answer it. The primary and most desirable skill and disposition in this step is the ability to respectfully speak back to sources and shape the conversation—for example, "That is interesting but, not related to my question."

Given the point of Step 3, you will not find instructions on the "right" way to do a literature review. That would be similar to telling students the right way to have a conversation about football. We do not supply a checklist that must be completed before you and your students can call your work a "literature review." Moreover, there are no "required" sources—such as academic articles or community members—that *must* be used to make something a research paper or literature review. Finally, there is no set amount of time you should devote to a literature review or a precise number of sources your students will have to find and converse with. Sarah, the teacher in the case study, and many others have done a literature review in two 50-minute class periods, because that was the time that was available. The right way to do a literature review is the way that allows students to actively and respectfully converse with sources in a manner that works for you. Our students have a lot of practice identifying relevant information and moving it to answer questions that have a right answer, and here we offer students the opportunity to develop the ability to engage with open-ended questions.

Conversations That Assess the Trustworthiness of a Source

Having a conversation with a source has many dimensions. Whether we are aware of it or not, we are assessing the accuracy and trustworthiness of the sources we converse with. This assessment is essentially an ethical task and part of the researcher's ethical obligation. The integrity of the research process and the ability of readers to have confidence in the conclusions that researchers reach is built on honesty and truthfulness. We have discussed ethics in terms of moral *reasoning* and the manner in which an ethical *perspective* can highlight what is good, just, and fair. Here, we introduce a third ethical dimension within *TfC* method, *obligation*: learning to meet the obligations spelled out in the researcher's professional code of ethics. This ethical obligation shapes the way researchers undertake many steps in the research process. We will return to this obligation in other steps in the *TfC* method. Here, the focus is on intellectual honesty.

In our discussion of framing research questions in Step 2, we have stressed the value of growing students that are alert to things that don't make sense or that seem strange. These same inquisitive qualities are also essential for discerning the truthfulness of sources. Indeed, students need to get into the habit, first, of spotting information that is simply wrong, claims that are exaggerated, or biases that distort or mislead and then investigating these instances and deciding if the data or source should be included in their literature review conversation.

As you give students more degrees of freedom in their choices, expect that some topics will surface that require further conversation. By having discussions about the importance of unbiased and accurate research, students get the hang of digging deeper to look for evidence for unsubstantiated information as well as for fake facts, agendas, and fear tactics.

For example, the Westchester (County) Joint Water Works (WJWW) asked a group of Valerie's students to investigate the origins of a series of articles that had appeared locally with titles such as *How Safe Is Your Drinking Water?* Valerie suggested that students contact an organization with an earth-friendly name that appeared in the article. The students investigated the funding sources for the organization and were amazed to discover that the organization was actually a marketing firm that placed scare articles along with associated product advertisements on the same webpage. These experiences, while unusual, were enormously helpful teaching moments and are especially useful given the vast amounts of information students have access to.

How to Have a Research Conversation

A research conversation requires that students remain focused on their research question and demonstrate humility and a willingness to learn. This kind of conversation honors the many voices who have contributed to building a body of knowledge, and uses questions to extend the understanding of everyone in the conversation. In public, we model this conversation and we help it along by asking students to be specific in how they express themselves.

Here are some excerpts from respectful conversations *TfC* students have had with human and written sources. Notice that the conversation with human sources are almost identical to those with written sources:

- "May I *shift the conversation back to our question* about teen employment by asking how you hire teenage employees for your business?"
- "*How does this census data speak to the question* of rural depopulation in our area?"
- "*Tell me more about what you mean* by community violence because that is what we are focusing on."
- "We have found many articles talking about how hard it is to enact policies that would address climate change. We need to *find more articles asking if it is fair or ethical to do nothing.*"
- "Maybe we *need to ask about that.*"
- "This article on single-parent families *doesn't fit with my experience.*"
- "*What would we have to believe* for that to be true?"
- "I never thought of that; maybe *we need to tweak our question.*"
- "*Until I read this study, I was so sure* that I wanted to do interviews. Now I realize a survey will be a better way to collect data on our question."

- "Let's record the citation for this article correctly so our *readers can better follow our work.*"
- *"These researchers had a similar research question* and found that teens who work less than 15 hours a week do just as well in school as those who don't work."
- "Let's make sure we have a focus group prompt that *tests the previous finding that was revealed through research with the high school students.*"

As the examples above suggest, a conversation requires give and take, questions and answers. In conversations, researchers (here, your students) have their question (or in some cases their perspective) in mind as their thinking evolves based on an increasingly sophisticated body of knowledge and an improved ability to evaluate information in relation to a question. After providing plenty of examples of what this conversation looks like, *TfC* teachers provide structured assignments that make it easy for students to begin having their own conversations with databases and sources.

Conversations with Databases. Our experiences have shown us that finding relevant resources for a literature review is one of the most difficult challenges students in high school and college face. The source of the difficulty lies in the fact that searching a database is a trial-and-error activity. Put another way, database searches can often be inefficient and frustrating, so practice is essential. Our students have struggled with basic searches, developing search terms, identifying relationships between different studies, and reporting what they have found.

There are many strategies to help students begin a database conversation. Valerie, in her curriculum and classes, has curated the process by beginning with sample articles. Then, the school librarian comes to Valerie's classes to teach students how to use this article to work backward and explore databases such as JSTOR (a data hub for research articles) and Noodle Tools, a research organization software application that gives students a structure and practice tracking and reflecting on their literature reviews. The students learn to generate search terms and identify field experts and community resources based on an initial article. The typical go-to resources she directs students toward are respected publications among communities of professionals (another example of conversing) and include research institutes such as Pew Research; publications such as *Scientific American, The New York Times, The New Yorker*; or come from think tanks such as The Brookings Institute.

Resource

Once students have been introduced to particular databases and alerted to reliable sources for research, they can begin their own conversations. This resource provides some ideas for these conversations.

Background for Teachers. Conversing with a database is an interactive process that is not the same as finding and downloading articles. Later on in this section, you will find hints for having this conversation. Prior to doing a database search with your students, we recommend that you do some searches yourself so that you can replicate the process in class. Try to remember your failures as well as successes. Then, allow your students to do some searches themselves.

Think and Act Like a Detective. Researchers need to be detectives. "People don't think searching databases is a creative act, but it is. In fact, looking for articles is like being a detective." To get started, here are two pieces of advice:

1. *Focus.* Many articles are interesting, but not relevant to your research question. The question is: Can a particular article help answer your research question? One way to get focused is to picture in your mind what the perfect article would look like. In other words, if you could magically create the article that would be most helpful to you and your class, what would it look like? Here is a scenario to give you an example of what we are talking about:
   - If a number of bikes have been stolen in Durham, North Carolina, and you wanted to recover them, what kind of an article would be most helpful?
   - The perfect article would discuss how someone found stolen bikes in your neighborhood or part of the city. This might not exist so you will want to find something as close to this as possible.
   - An article that focuses on recovering a bike (or something similar to a bike) in a neighborhood that is similar to yours, that has similar demographics, would probably be helpful.
   - If an article like that doesn't exist, the next best thing might be an article on recovering bikes in a small American city or, even better, an article that talks about what people who recovered bikes in small cities across America have learned.
   - As you sit looking at your database, you have the perfect article in your mind's eye. But know too that it is quite likely that the perfect article may not exist and so you will want to collect articles that are *as close* to that perfect article as possible.
2. *Play the Detective.* The best detectives try to get into the heads of bad guys so they can understand them and even anticipate what they did or will do next. You want to be a database detective. There are many databases; each has its own unique system for storing articles. Your task is to get into the heads of the people who designed the filing system for the database you are looking at.
   - Think of finding articles in a database as being a little like finding a pair of shoes in an aunt's old house. Given her quirky personality, where would she put them? (We told you research was a creative act.)

- Before starting to sneeze from the dust in your aunt's closet, you realize that your best bet is to make finding them an interactive process that is going to work by trial and error. The interactions between you and your aunt might provide some clues, but her memory is not what it once was and she has no real idea where they are, except that they are red with a heel. So, you have to outsmart the problem.
- You look in the bedroom closet—you find handbags and no shoes—so, you refine your search. You have a list of possible places (suggested by your aunt with your help) and you check off bedroom closet. The best way to make sure you are focused is to record your search (terms) as you go.
- Suddenly, it hits you. Everything in your aunt's house is color-coded. The kitchen is full of yellow dishes, the living room is blue. You search for the color red and, lo and behold, you find red items in the attic. Once there, you head for a closet that has a sign on it that says "wearables." Remember you get better with practice.

Students' ideas on approaching databases like detectives:
1. *Keep a record* of your searches and the search terms you have used so you will work efficiently. Database searches are challenging enough without repeating yourself.
2. *Limit* the search by: (1) kind of source—articles; (2) language—English; and/or (3) dates—start by limiting your search to articles published in the last 2 years.
3. *Brainstorm synonyms*—get into the mind of the search engine, and try to brainstorm the words (search terms) under which the articles you want will be grouped. If you are looking for articles on lowering the voting age, you might try: "youth and voting," "teens and suffrage," "young adults and voting reform," and so on.
4. *Continue to try* search terms until you get a manageable number of results. Again, record all the terms you have tried.
5. Our rule is *no more than 40* is a good number of results for a search— that is, if you get 3,000 results with a search term, record it and then try another more specific term.
6. *Ruthlessly eliminate—converse* with the title and the abstract. Interesting is not good enough. Nor is somewhat related: If you are interested in teen- agers and voting, an article with voting in the title or teenager in the title is not close enough. You want an article with *both* in the title. Get as close as you can to the perfect. If you are unsure about an article after you have had a conversation with it, take a closer look at the whole article.
7. Once you find a good article, *locate the "keywords" or "subjects"* in the entry as these will tell you the terms that the database uses to organize similar articles. (Some databases will provide this information under the heading:

"similar searches.") Use them! They will help you efficiently find relevant articles.

8. Add your own search ideas to this list.

Conversations with Sources. There are a handful of basic questions your students should ask the sources they are working with. Here are some examples of questions that students in a semester or yearlong research project might "ask" a source:

- *Does the article provide critical background information?* For example, a class considering the advantages of lowering the voting age for local elections would be interested to know if any towns have already lowered the voting age for local elections.
- *Does the article help you tweak your research question or develop a hypothesis on how to answer the question that you could test the next step in the TfC research method?*
- *Do you and your students need to refine your research question?* For example, are your fellow researchers (the authors of the research articles you have seen) using a different word for the issue you are interested in— employment instead of jobs? If yes, do you want to change the wording of your question slightly so that you can more easily build on existing work and contribute to future researchers?
- *Can the article help you and your students design your own empirical research?* In the next few weeks, you and your students will design your own research. The class is going to choose a method to collect your data— interviews, focus groups, surveys, and so on—and decide what population you should interview or survey. You can learn a lot from the research design choices previous researchers have made. If a particular method worked well, you might try that method *and* ensure that your research is distinctive by asking different questions or looking at a different population—young people instead of adults. Alternatively, if most researchers are using surveys and interviews, you might try focus groups to get a different perspective on the issue.
- *Does the article alert you and your student to possible or surprising findings you should be on the lookout for when you analyze your data?* What did previous researchers who looked at questions like yours find? You should keep these findings in mind when you complete your research so that you can compare your findings to theirs. Will your findings support previous research or will they be contrary to be existing knowledge and thus be surprising?

Keeping a Record of Conversations with Sources. Sarah, the teacher in the case study, wisely had her students create a written or digital record of their conversations so that they could later be the basis for a research paper/presentation or literature review section of an assignment. Part of the work of conversing with a source is to properly cite the source and succinctly list what has been learned from the source that is directly relevant to the research question.

Valerie has her students use research software (Noodle Tools) to record sources, citations, quotes, and research notes, or she has her students create their own databases for the same purposes. (If your students are creating their own databases [i.e. a spreadsheet], remind them to copy the URL, article title, author, retrieval date, and time, or if there is none, a sponsoring organization.) Then, students copy and paste relevant quotes that might be used as supporting evidence in a report. Last and most importantly, students describe what their conversation produced. Ideally, they should write a few sentences that explain the relevance of the source to the research question—why it was chosen, and a few specific ways that the information addresses the research question.

Resource

Here is a record of what a student's conversation with a source might look like:

Smith, Joe. (2015). *Civic Engagement in Suburban America*. The Journal of Civil Discourse. Any Town Publishing Company. Chicago, Illinois. Volume 3. Pages 17–23. Retrieved: 09/29/19 at 10:00 am http://www.civicsinamerica.org

Our research question is: "What is the Relationship between Civic Engagement and Social Media?

This article is an analysis of government efforts to utilize social media and networking sources to engage younger generations and increase their political participation. The study used a specific layout that measured how people who wanted to be politically active searched and found information involving their governments through social media and social networking. Different technologies were incorporated to see the impact of all different forms of media. (I wonder if we could design something like this for our research.) The study had two major results that are relevant to our research questions. The first was that searching via social media and networking is affected by the searcher, their interests, and their politics. . . .

From Research Conversations to Research Papers and Literature Reviews.
The teachers we have worked with have presented the conversations their students have had with sources in two primary ways: (1) as short research papers or presentations in which an open-ended question that emerges from the curriculum is answered; and (2) as a literature review section either for a semester or yearlong *TfC* research paper/presentation or to provide greater analytical rigor to a PBL, service-learning, experiential education project.

Short *TfC* research papers and literature reviews are more similar than different. Both begin with an open-ended research question and, most importantly, both are focused on conversations with sources. The differences between the two lies in the purpose of the conversation.

Short TfC Research Papers. The purpose of a short curricular-based *TfC* research paper is to answer an open-ended question. For teachers who have routinely set research papers focused on identifying, moving, and organizing information to answer specific prompts from a set of articles, we suggest you periodically assign a research paper that helps students learn to have conversations with sources. Social studies disciplines are oriented around longstanding research questions, and much research is produced to answer these questions—for example, did the New Deal end the Depression? These are ideal questions to begin with or refine for research papers. In addition, Step 2 of this guide provides suggestions and examples of how to move from interesting issues and topics to effective research questions for curricular inquiry and exploration.

Finally, "essential questions" that ask why or explore relationships and are part of a prewritten curriculum, often make good research questions. Essential questions appear in a broad spectrum of curriculum designs and vary in quality and focus. Our advice is to analyze the degrees of freedom an essential question offers your students and to either use them as is or as a basis for differentiating curriculum between students who are eager for open-ended questions of their own design and those who are still grappling with comparisons or other more concrete aspects of exploration.

Literature Review Sections of Research Reports. If your students are writing a literature review as part of a research project, they will already have a question. Here, the purpose of the literature review section is to learn from others how best to answer this question—to learn, for example, whether the question needs to be tweaked, what population should research subjects be drawn from (for example, people registered to vote or all adults eligible to vote), what data collection methods might be best (surveys, interviews, focus groups, and so on), and how previous researchers have answered the question.

Resource

How to Structure a Short TfC Research Paper/Presentation or a Literature Review Section. Here, we offer a basic outline that can help students write either research papers/presentations or literature review sections of research reports or presentations. There are three parts to the process and each may be modeled in class discussions, accomplished in groups, or individually, and/or assigned for verbal or written presentations. A short *TfC* research paper is usually assigned as an end in itself, and a literature review is generally the foundation for a longer investigation. In either case, the process is largely the same. However, a literature review for a community or long-term project will include more detail and resources.

The three parts of this assignment are:

1. *Introduction*. Introducing the research question—background information so the reader can understand the question and discussion of why this question is important.
2. *Discussion*. Relating the research question to the research areas that are relevant and organizing the conversations students have had with the sources (human and published) in these areas.
3. *Conclusion*. Concluding with a brief verbal or written discussion about how the sources your students have conversed with have, together, helped approach and answer the research question.

Here is what these three parts look like in a *TfC* literature review:

1. Introduction Section. What is the research question?

How do community organizations address hunger in the Town of Rye and Westchester County in today's challenging environment?

Why is this important?

The overwhelming majority of U.S. households have a stable food supply. However, about 15% of households in America suffer from food insecurity. Perhaps even more troubling, 10% of households with children in America have an insufficient food supply to some degree. The national figure of 15% may not seem to be a large number. However, to put this figure in perspective, the same number of people who went without food consistently was roughly equivalent to the number of people who lived in Connecticut, Iowa, Mississippi, Arkansas, Utah, Kansas, and Nevada combined.

For whom and in what context does the research question matter?

This report focuses on hunger in Westchester County, New York, and in the Town of Rye, in particular. Some of us have volunteered in soup kitchens and food pantries in the area. The knowledge we gained from these experiences and our preliminary research has encouraged us to undertake analytical work to supplement our volunteering. We have come to understand the variety of challenges hunger poses to individuals and communities and have learned about the range of organizations that exist to address food insecurity in the area.

2. Discussion Section. This section connects the research question to existing and related research. This helps students see how being part of the research club can help them answer their own questions.

This work of connecting begins with a paragraph that identifies what research areas will be discussed and how they relate to the research question. The ability to not just summarize relevant areas, but relate them to the research question, is the critical skill to be developed.

Our research question exists at the intersection of three topics: Food insecurity in America and Westchester County; national and local programs to reduce food insecurity; how area food banks, food pantries, and community kitchens have been responding to food insecurity.

Below is the section of the discussion that focuses on "Area food banks, food pantries, and community kitchens." Note, that this section is not an information dump, but is instead shaped and edited to speak directly to the research question. For example, in the last paragraph, Hamlin County, Ohio, is discussed because it is a model for how groups and organizations can relate to one another—that is, it speaks directly to the research question that animated the paper/presentation.

Area Food Banks, Food Pantries, and Community Kitchens as Responses to Food Insecurity: There are seven food pantries and four soup kitchens serving meals and distributing food to residents of the Town of Rye. At least one food pantry is available every day except Sunday. At least one soup kitchen is available every day except Saturday. They serve all who come. Individual pantries and soup kitchens vary in the number of people they serve from 30 to several hundred and their frequency of service. They also serve slightly different demographics, although all mention that their clientele includes at least some Hispanic residents. The Westchester County Food Bank, which provides the bulk of the food for these community organizations, does not require that receiving organizations ask for personal information from patrons. However, they do suggest some guidelines for the kinds of information that might be requested.

According to recent interviews conducted by Dave Thomas and Greg Arcaro of the Town of Rye, leaders of food pantries and community kitchens in the area have a clear idea of the challenges facing them. Three in particular were highlighted in the preliminary report written by the town: shortage of food donations, shortage of volunteers, and at least one organization mentioned that signage and additional publicity was needed so that people would know what food-related services were available. For example, representatives of the St. Thomas Food Pantry state that they could use help when it comes to food and other donations that they receive.

These leaders expressed concerns about another shortage. Many mentioned a need for more volunteers to fulfill their basic mission. Running through these shortages may be a publicity issue. Does the community know more food is needed to feed the hungry or that the community needs more volunteers? Further, one organization highlighted the need to publicize the availability of food via pantries and kitchens in the area. Finally, these leaders wondered where does a community organization go when it is has a problem—such as a stove that doesn't work?

Westchester County is not, of course, the only county in America dealing with food insecurity issues. What are some of these other countries doing? To answer this question, we looked at Hamilton County in Ohio, which has become a leader in county-level approaches to hunger and resembles Westchester County in terms of its racial and economic diversity. What distinguishes Hamilton County is the way that critical information is shared between social service organizations within the community and how activities are coordinated. For example, economies of scale are realized through pooling resources and sharing assets such as trucks and manpower. In addition, by distributing responsibility for distinct populations such as those for immigrants or families, Hamilton County community's food pantries communicate with soup kitchens and form community service relationships between organizations. Those relationships have been integral to Hamilton County's success in battling hunger and may be a source from which Westchester County's organizers may draw ideas and strategies.

3. Conclusion Section. This section summarizes what was learned from conversing with sources that can help either answer the research question (for short research papers) or shape the research project going forward (for semester or yearlong research projects). Below, you will find the conclusion section of the literature review quoted above. It illustrates how a literature review can shape the data collection stage of a semester or yearlong research project.

We frequently read and heard about the challenges that organizations across America have in collecting food. Our literature review revealed that interviews conducted by the officials of the Town of Rye highlighted these same challenges here in Westchester County. This led our focus group facilitators to ask direct and detailed questions about how food resources are obtained and allocated. These prompts, in turn, produced important findings. We learned that many times, donated food is not picked up on time by the designated organization and that there is no system in place to alert another organization who may be able to take the place of the previously scheduled party. We also learned that there is a shortage of drivers and vehicles that gather and dispense available food in the community. This tells us something important about how local organizations are addressing food insecurity.

TEACHING

Over the years we, and the teachers we have worked with, have developed a cluster of insights that can help teachers assist students to have conversations with sources and present these conversations in papers and presentations.

First, whether your students are writing a short curricular-based research paper or a literature review section for a semester or yearlong research project, we suggest that you curate the process so students can focus on the challenging and exciting skill of conversing with sources. Thus, we suggest that you limit the number of databases your students will need to consult and/or the number and kind of sources they should consult, and/or how they should engage with these sources.

The idea that high school students can be part of the research club and contribute to a research tradition is largely foreign to the high school curriculum right through the AP gauntlet. Having students understand that they are embarking on work that matters in a larger academic arena and, more importantly, in the world, is enormously enlivening. The dawning of the transitional thinking from passive vessel to engaged creator needs to be acknowledged by you and celebrated. However, getting there requires that you employ your curatorial powers to guide students as they build research skills and bring projects to completion under time constraints. We urge a deductive planning approach where the teacher decides on her own, or in carefully framed conversations with students, what the key topics/sections of the research paper or literature review will be and then identifies databases to consult and/or sources under each topic for students to converse with.

Second, we think of ourselves not as teachers but as senior researchers or lab directors, and we suggest that you present yourself to your class in the same way. The redefinition of our roles, from teacher to senior researcher or lab director, fundamentally redefines the classroom dynamics because it says: We are on the same team with different levels of experience. This simple shift is enormously helpful in moving you from the position of sage-on-the-stage to guide-on-the-side. As much as possible, you want to be leading and modeling the research process. For example, when working with a student on individual research, try to show, not tell. Ask yourself what you would do if you were tackling your student's question. "Here is the first place I would look to get information to answer that question, where would you look next?" "Here are the things I would want to know. What do you want to know?" The best teaching here is from within the method or, more specifically, from *within* a research conversation. Moreover, in most cases, special knowledge of the question a student is exploring is not necessary; you most likely possess experiences that will inform your intuition.

Third, conversing with sources is both essential for good research and one of the most creative aspects of the research process. Some students find that the concept of conversing is strange and may be averse to it, because they have never done it and it is always challenging to try new things. To reinforce relevance, we relate the literature review process to what happens in college and workplaces to help teens get over the hump that new thinking presents when they (often) perceive learning in school as unrelated to the real world.

Fourth, as with other thinking and doing in the *TfC* method, having productive conversations with sources takes practice or, in the language of sports, "reps." Progress will occur in small steps and the skill is best developed in a recursive manner. The secret is to keep offering students opportunities to have conversations. Be sure to affirm, encourage, and build on even the smallest beginnings of a conversation. When a student said, "My teammates and our coach would never agree with that statement," this is a start. The teacher answered: "That is what I am talking about. . . ." "Why would your team never agree with that statement?" "Maybe in discussing that statement in your paper, you will want to mention that there is some basis to dispute it or disagree with the statement, laying out your views. What we have now may not be the best or only answer to our question."

ASSESSMENT

Formative Assessment

Self-Assessment. Students find it helpful to see the final work product that is associated with each step so they can see where they can contribute, what might be challenging, and what they will need to learn.

In Step 3, to give students a sense of what conversing with sources looks like, we suggest that you have each student read a first draft of a literature review produced by an expert researcher, other *TfC* students, and/or a college student (available on the resource page of the *TfC* website). Then, have students answer some of the following questions:

1. How does a literature review help answer our research question?
2. Does this literature review remind you of anything you have read or seen before?
3. Listed below are tasks related to writing a research paper and/or doing a literature review section. Circle the parts of the literature review process that are listed below in which you are able to make the biggest contribution:
   a. Finding articles or people we should talk to.
   b. Having a conversation with a person or article to get information that can help us answer our question.
   c. Developing an outline for our literature review.
   d. Editing the work of other students to create a first draft of our literature review.
4. What will be the most challenging aspect of the literature review/research report for you personally (use the answer options in Question 3)?

Teacher Assessment. We have found it helpful for students to keep research journals and to give examples of the thinking and doing we are focusing on in Step 3—for example, brainstorming a list of people in the community to talk to. Here is a prompt to give students practice at the thinking and doing associated with this literature review step—such as identifying and conversing with sources that can help you address a challenge or answer a question.

Pretend you are interviewing for a job at a local business. Identify a specific business that hires young people. Brainstorm three lists:

a. List all of the people you and others in your life might know who have worked for the business.
b. List people who might be able to help you prepare for this job interview—such as current employees you might know.
c. List three questions you would ask these people to help you prepare for your interview.

Individual Assignments:
- After in-class demonstration guided by the resource on how to have a conversation with a database (above), have students use the prompts to find two articles that are relevant to their research question.
- After examining the resource illustrating how to have a conversation with an academic article (above), assign students an article and ask them to write a list of "interview" questions and answers for the article's author.

Summative Assessment

Conversations with Sources. After teaching students how to have a conversation with a source using the resource above, read examples of conversations other students have had with an academic article, and then ask your students to write about a conversation with one source that was relevant to their research question.

Performance Tasks. Social science research is a social activity. It involves talking to sources and then sharing these conversations with other researchers, community members, leaders of organizations, and government officials who will find this information helpful for their lives and work. This sharing must be done in a clear, concise, and accessible manner so that audiences can easily benefit from the research of your students in the course of their busy work lives. These two performance tasks were developed to enable a teacher to assess the ability of students to share their conversations with others.

Individual Performance Task*:* Here, the audience is the other researchers in the class.

Imagine the article or data you have looked at could speak back:
- Develop a set of questions you want to ask this document, and write your questions and the answers the document gave you.
- Make a 2-minute presentation to the class discussing what source—human, documentaries, and so on—you (or your group) conversed with and what you have learned from these conversations that may help answer your question.

Group Performance Task: Here, the audience is an organization in the community that could benefit from a conversation your students are having with research articles, but would never think to ask. People who run nonprofit organizations or government offices are so busy with the day-to-day tasks that they often have no time to read new research that discusses innovations that organizations, such as theirs, have developed to address common problems—for example, at Duke, Bill's students created a memo for school officials that illustrated new ideas for how to solve a growing problem: *How do school districts provide translation and interpretation services for students and families whose first language is not English and in a manner that meets federal legal obligations and is cost-effective?*

A brief, (grammatically) clean, and concise memo highlighting trends in research and practice would be very welcome to many practitioners. This performance task is focused on developing such a memo and in the process building a relationship that might be helpful later in research process, specifically in Step 7, where students use their research findings to collaboratively address the underlying community challenge.

- Identify a nonprofit or government agency that is working in the area where your research question lies and learn what they do. For example, if you are focusing on hunger, a food pantry or soup kitchen might be a good choice.
- Write a two- to three-page memo to the director of this organization that describes what your class learned in their "conversations" on this issue and, if possible, discuss how this learning would help the organization perform its mission.
- Invite a field expert in a topic of interest for an in-class interview. Ask the interviewee about organizational or community challenges that they think are important. Have the class create a literature review that addresses an issue raised and present it to the organization.

Making Curricular Connections

Social Studies Connections. In world history and U.S. history classes, students are often asked to assess conflicting historical accounts. This task has a parallel in almost every field. In social science, the literature review is a place where a researcher discusses competing claims or theories with an eye to testing the claims in their own research. Note, that seeing connections between disciplines and fields encourages students to begin to think and do in an interdisciplinary manner. The ability to use two disciplines to address a puzzle or challenge is the most impressive thing an undergraduate can do.

Discussions or Short Written Assignments: Historians (who may ask about the long-term causes of food insecurity in the United States) and social scientists (who may ask about the relationship between race and food insecurity in the United States) often disagree among themselves.

Respond to the following questions:

- In what ways might historians and sociologists use new data they have collected to help resolve disagreements?
- What is the best way to write the conclusion of a report/literature review when there is no agreement about how to answer the research question?

FREQUENTLY ASKED QUESTIONS

Q: I have tried everything but can't get some of my students to begin a conversation with a source. What do I do?

A: Try making it personal. Encourage students to use their perspectives—if they have developed them earlier in the research process—to initiate conversations with sources. Ask: Does this census data about our town make sense given your experiences? Why or why not? Does this explanation of the causes of poverty square with your experiences? If your students haven't surfaced their own perspectives, use the language of "you." You are an intelligent person, does this data surprise you, make sense to you? Is this true given your life and that of your family?

Then, remind students that this is what researchers are doing when they interact with other researchers: They are asking their fellow researchers questions and seeing if what they say makes sense and helps them answer other questions they may have.

Q: What is the difference between an interview with a wise community member as part of a literature review and an interview with a community member in the data collection step (Step 6) later in a semester or yearlong *TfC* research project?

A: When an interview is conducted in the literature review step, it is primarily intended to get suggestions and ideas for improving the research process itself. As part of a literature review, you might ask: Do you think we are asking the right question? What methods have you used to get data on this question—indeed, is an interview the right method in your opinion? What advice would you give us in approaching community members about this topic? An interview conducted in the data collection research stage (Step 6) is designed to answer the research question. Having said that, many teachers have used interviews in the literature review step to *model* the respect and focus that an interview requires as well as the logistical tasks involved in scheduling an interview.

Q: How do you know when to stop identifying and conversing with sources?

A: If time is not a factor—and when is it not?—this step of the research process can be brought to a close when your students are seeing the same articles again and again in their searches and/or hearing and reading the same information from multiple sources. This is evidence that you are ready to organize and write up your literature review.

As we have suggested above, it is always more than fine to shorten this step so that it works for you and your class. This is a typical teacher comment: "We will devote two classes to this work; let's see how much practice students can get conversing with sources in this time." Again, researchers everywhere are always working under constraints.

eTOOLBOX: RESOURCES

A range of resources for this step—including, hints, activities, lecture outlines, and samples of student work—may be found on the resource page of the *TfC* website: https://www.tools4changeseminar.com/resources.html

Design
Developing a Plan to Collect Data to Answer a Research Question

Middle and high school students are often recognized for their youthful passion, energy, and commitment. They are rarely, however, singled out for their ability to bring knowledge to bear on problems in their school and community. When students collect data that, for example, sheds light on how people move from concern about sustainability to action, they gain authority in the community. When they undertake short research exercises to inquire into questions in the curriculum, they gain authority in the classroom and in relationship to the curriculum. For example, students in a U.S. history class developed their own knowledge of the Great Depression by conducting a two-question interview with older residents in their community to determine if their memories of the 1930s shape how they view money and debt today.

Empirical research involves collecting new data to answer questions. *TfC* empirical research design can help you and your students plan and undertake short and concise "tests" of the curriculum and organize and execute larger data collection efforts that answer a community research question or guide field research in PBL, experiential, or service-learning projects.

CASE STUDY

An interdistrict *TfC* class was intrigued by a puzzle that Valerie's students in the Rye Neck High School *TfC* had uncovered in survey research a year earlier. In this earlier research, respondents consistently said they were very concerned about climate change, but they also reported that they felt powerless to do anything about it. How, the interdistrict students asked, do people move from anxiety about sustainability to action? This became the first draft of their research question. The students in the interdistrict program decided that the best way to answer this question was to talk to leaders of local NGOs focused on sustainability and government officials charged with encouraging citizens and businesses to voluntarily adopt sustainable practices. These leaders, it was thought, could speak from actual experience about how to successfully move people from concern to action in the areas of climate change and sustainability.

The class decided that a short open-ended interview would be most effective because it would enable these leaders and officials to describe what was essentially a process. Students identified 10 to 15 county leaders, inside and outside of government, and developed and tested a short five-question interview protocol. The interview protocol was assessed both in terms of the informational value of each question and with an eye toward ensuring that answers could be displayed in frequency tables to aid future analysis. (The group hoped that the protocol could be used for interviews with hundreds of leaders over time.) The goal was to encourage the interview teams to resourcefully collect small amounts of data that would be aggregated and reviewed based on what they had learned about statistics in their mathematics classes.

The students accessed family networks and looked online for organizations and contact information for the leaders. They then scripted their introductions, honed their interview skills, and were given several days to return to class with the answers to their survey questions and the notes they had taken during their conversations. The challenge for the students was to consider all responses as empirical data—both the original survey responses that inspired the new research and the more detailed explanations of the process by which volunteers and/or citizens became active. In this way, the *TfC* students in the interdistrict group moved beyond a simple Google Forms survey to a much richer research process that combined larger survey trends with the more nuanced explanations that the open-ended interview questions yielded. These design decisions led to several interesting class discussions about how in-depth interviews can sometimes solve puzzles that survey data reveal.

KEY FEATURES

Today, we create online surveys for every occasion. However, we rarely ask the most basic questions: (1) Is an online survey the best data collection method for the job?; (2) If it is, have we developed an effective and ethical survey instrument?; and (3) How will the survey responses be analyzed after they are collected? In a word, what is so often missing in our enthusiasm for online surveys is deliberative research design.

The collection and analysis of data yields new knowledge. However, modest it may be, this knowledge can enrich the curriculum and improve the communities we live in. Research that brings new knowledge to bear isn't an activity only for PhDs in a university lab, it is also something you and your students can and should do in the classroom and in the community.

The key thinking and doing in this step are captured by the verb "design." Designing effective research is a process that is informed by the experiences of previous researchers and the application of well-established techniques—for example, how to write effective focus group prompts. There are two specific aspects to this design work. The first task is to make informed, although not necessarily long and involved, decisions about which qualitative method(s)—interviews, focus groups, surveys, and participant observation—will allow you to test a curricular issue or answer your research question within your circumstances and constraints. The second task is to create research tools that work—such as developing effective surveys, focus group prompts, and/or interview questionnaires to fit your needs.

PLANNING

TfC research design begins with a research question. However, a key part of the research design planning process involves honestly assessing existing circumstances, constraints, and resources. Research must always conform to the context in which it is undertaken. This is especially true of teachers who want to undertake brief curricular-inspired data collection forays to develop new knowledge to engage students. But it is also true of teachers who plan semester or yearlong *TfC* community research projects. It is important to remember that the directors of university-based research labs also have to tailor research to existing resources and constraints—budgets, lab space, and so on.

In a perfect world, we would always get a statistically significant sample. Few researchers—who do not have grants or research accounts—have the time and money to do this. For you and your students, other constraints will include the time you have for data collection, support available to manage the logistics involved with some methods, and your own learning goals. The planning challenge in Step 4 is to thoughtfully balance the ideal research design with what is possible for you and your students. This balance is easier to strike if you remember the goal here is to have your students try their hand at empirical research and learn how data can deepen understanding and bring authority to everyday life.

Deliberative Research Design. Deliberative here means understanding the advantages and disadvantages of each decision you and your students make. The goal should be to express this understanding in no more than two sentences. After two sentences, people simply stop reading and start skimming. This will take practice, but it is a worthwhile aspiration. Here is an example of an effective two-sentence design decision by a Duke University undergraduate:

> "We were interested in private feelings about faith and cancer recovery and chose in-depth interviews because the open-ended and relatively unstructured nature of this data collection method makes it easier for people to discuss their feelings. The time I have available for this research will allow me to interview six people."

Notice, that making a two-sentence argument does not require special knowledge and technical language, or an "A" average. We have found that balancing the advantages and disadvantages involved in making research decisions is a skill that can be cultivated. You and your students will get better at this skill with experience. The best way to start cultivating this skill is to become familiar with the basic types of design decisions that researchers make, study how researchers have made these decisions in the past, and have you and your students start making them yourselves.

Research Design Decisions

Here are three decisions that researchers typically make, followed by examples of how *TfC* students have made these decisions.

Decision 1: Which people or organizations would most effectively help you answer your research question? Given your question, what types of people or organizations could best provide an answer—for example, people of a certain age, neighborhood or region, race, income, or another factor that defines a group we may be interested in.

Student rationales:
- "We are interested in voting behavior so we probably want to focus on people who are eligible to vote or people who are registered to vote. It seems more interesting to understand why people who are registered don't vote because they have demonstrated interest in participating in the political process."
- "There is lots of information about two-parent families; maybe we want to focus on families of all kinds."
- "We want to know if taxes on gas are fair; we need to find drivers, ideally from different income groups."
- "We don't want to make our classmates (or their parents) who may be hungry themselves uncomfortable, so it may make sense to focus our research on people who run food pantries and soup kitchens."
- "Okay, we know we want to focus on single parents. But we need to think about where we can find single parents."
- "Everyone drinks water and some people use water filters. We need to collect survey responses at the library and at the supermarket where we will meet a range of people and get the most diverse responses we can."

Decision 2: Would our data be most compelling if we question people or observe them? Given what you know about the question you want to answer, do you want to ask/speak to people or observe them? The most commonly used methods for asking/speaking include: surveys, focus groups, interviews, and participant observation.

Student Rationales:
- "Even if we are looking for the same things, each of us will see the situation differently; surveys are less subjective; I think we should go with them."

- "We are focused on social media usage; it is not possible for our class to observe people using social media, so we will have to just asked them to tell us what they do by using a survey."
- "Maybe we could we show a very short video that would demonstrate the harm that could potentially be done by solar geoengineering and then watch people's faces to see if they thought this was a good thing to do? This is certainly possible, but we would need to make big assumptions when we guess what people's faces are telling us."

Resource: Overview of Primary Data Collection Methods

Survey—Brief (5–10 minute) oral or written questionnaires, usually with a limited number of answer options.
- *Advantages*—Inexpensive, easy to administer and analyze (especially via online surveys like Google Forms and Survey Monkey, which we would strongly recommend) and thus, ideal for getting large numbers of respondents.
- *Disadvantages*—When an answer is either unclear or interesting, there is no way to follow up with the respondent; nor can you ask for clarification. Not a good method for questions that require original thinking or involve complex issues or feelings.
- *Sample research topics suitable for a survey method*—Voter attitudes, civic engagement, refugees' use of transportation, teen employment status.

Focus group—Small group discussions, carefully moderated so as to focus on your research question.
- *Advantages*—Makes detailed, spontaneous, and surprising answers possible; a group setting allows participants to make connections that they would be unable to make on their own and makes it possible for a group to amplify points, agree, and disagree.
- *Disadvantages*—Strong personalities can dominate, leading to "group think"; can be logistically challenging—such as coordinating the schedules of 5–12 people; requires vigilance to ensure a productive and safe environment for honest discussion.
- *Sample research topic suitable for focus group method*—Does the size of the organization affect the challenges that hunger relief organizations face and how they deal with them?

Participant observation—Structured observation of a social environment—such as people interacting in a space.
- *Advantages*—Allows researcher to go beyond what people say they do and observe how they actually behave; especially helpful with sensitive research questions that people may find it difficult to answer honestly—for example, do students in our school self-segregate by race?

- *Disadvantages*—Time-consuming; observations can be subjective and thus difficult to analyze, especially when you have several researchers observing the same event.
- *Sample research topics suitable for participant observation method*—How does gender influence teen friendships? What is the relationship between race and where students sit in the cafeteria during lunch?

In-depth interview—An in-depth, structured, and focused conversation usually with one person.
- *Advantages*—Allows for in-depth answers and opportunities to follow up for clarification and deeper understanding; especially good with research questions whose answers are difficult or complicated to explain, based on feelings, still evolving, and/or likely to vary greatly among research subjects.
- *Disadvantages*—The personal and labor-intensive nature of this method means only a small number of people can be interviewed; subjective nature of the method can make it hard to analyze.
- *Sample research topics*—The effect of religious belief on cancer patients? How women balance family and career aspirations in the course of a week?

Decision 3: If questioning people, what method will be most effective?

Given what you now know about your research question, what is the best method or methods for gleaning information from the people you are interested in speaking with—should you use surveys, focus groups, and/or depth interviews?

Student Rationales:
- "Both in-depth interviews with food pantry leaders and a focus group made up of the same people would give us the information we need. But, arranging and transcribing 10 in-depth interviews would take more time than we have available. Let's do the focus group."
- "Could we just have each student find out the price of three basic items—for example, a gallon of milk—in the store in which their family shops to understand how zip codes might affect the cost of living?"
- "The police department has their own survey of community safety. I wonder if we want to use some of their survey questions (and, of course, acknowledge this) in our own research to see if we get different answers when our class asks the questions."
- "We could get a sense of people's general attitude in regard to allowing 16-year-olds to vote and then run a focus group or two to examine these attitudes more closely. But do we have time for both?"

Resource

Here is a short exercise to give students practice selecting an appropriate method to answer their research question: For each of the following questions, choose the best method to answer the research question *or* write a research question that fits the method given.

1. Research question: How do religious beliefs impact the policies of our living presidents?
   - Method:
   - Write one sentence that convinces someone you chose the best method:
2. Research question: How do drug dealers live their lives?
   - Method:
   - Write one sentence that convinces someone you chose the best method:
3. You have been given $100,000 to use the focus group research method to answer a research question.
   - Come up with a research question so you can get the money.
   - Write one sentence that convinces someone else that your research question is a good fit for the focus group method:

Building Research Tools

Once decisions have been made about the design of your research, you and your students will want to create the tools (surveys, questionnaires, interview questions, observational checklists, and so on) that will enable you to do this work. While it doesn't make sense to say that there is a "wrong" survey question, there are many survey questions and focus group prompts that are simply not effective.

Survey questions or focus group prompts that are ineffective are confusing, offensive, or biased. They prevent people who wish to honestly answer your questions from doing so. Survey questions or focus group prompts that work look a certain way and have similar characteristics. This point might be reduced to: the words you use matter. Many students have had exposure to Internet plagiarism and media bias. Sensitivity to the ways that words may bias responses is an aspect of the ethical obligations that come with doing research. Just as researchers are expected to ensure that the literature that they cite is accurate (Step 3), they are also expected to conduct their own research in a manner that minimizes bias. We have found that connecting the development of research tools to this larger ethical obligation helps remind students that creating survey questions that are fair and unbiased is part of their job as a researcher.

Creating an effective survey doesn't require high test scores or special knowledge. Instead, it simply requires having a sense of people and the ability to write effective questions and answer options. The best way to gain proficiency at this skill is by first looking at the work of experienced researchers who have developed time-tested strategies for creating questions or prompts, studying examples of effective research tools, and then having your students make their own tools through trial and error.

As a teacher, it will be necessary for you to curate print or online resources that provide guidance on question development for the type or types of research tools that your class decides to create. At this vital point in the research process, students may need to be reminded that, because of their age and out of respect for those they wish to study, it is necessary to strike a balance between tact and respect, on the one hand, and the desirability of obtaining necessary information, on the other. For example, adults do not generally like to be asked how much they earn. Young researchers may not know how else to ask for sensitive, but important information like income and so they will need your help. This is especially true in a focus group—whereas, in an anonymous survey, asking for a check mark next to an income range may be appropriate. For these reasons, we have included some issues that you and your students might consider in developing survey/interview questions and/or focus group prompts:

- Is the question relevant? Does it provide information that is directly relevant to an aspect of the research question?
- Is the question so vague and answer options so open-ended that respondents either can unintentionally or intentionally evade the question or provide answers that are too general to be helpful or too random to be analyzed? As a rule of thumb for surveys, it is best to limit answer options to no more than three or four and offer "other" (or fill in the blank) as an option only where you are not confident your answer options are not capturing the most common likely answers.
- Does the question ask people to recall events, people, or places that may distract them from providing the information you most want?
- Is the question asking people to provide sensitive information—such as information of a personal nature or in regard to illegal activity?
- Once a survey is created, do you want a physical survey or an online format? We strongly recommend an online survey as they are much easier to collect and analyze. But there are situations where a physical survey is the better option because it will dramatically increase responses. For example, when a group of Valerie's students collected data on Hispanic immigrants' access to transportation (a sensitive issue due to the possibility of a respondent being undocumented), the students worked with the staff of the local Community Resource Center. The staff recommended a paper-and-pencil survey because they were convinced that respondents might not be comfortable with an online format.

Two Research Design Challenges

Teachers have made the three research design decisions above and developed corresponding research tools in undertaking two primary research assignments:

1. Short, discrete empirical research forays that bring new knowledge to bear on the curriculum.

2. As the research design step in a semester or yearlong *TfC* community research project or as a resource for planning the field research component of PBL, service-learning, experiential education project.

Empirical Research in Content Curriculum. Empirical research—in other words, inquiry that involves collecting new data—can provide students with new angles for engaging with issues, concepts, puzzles, and questions in the curriculum. These angles of engagement are distinctly different from writing a standard research paper or participating in a debate and, thus, they offer new ways to make the curriculum relevant. These short research experiments can be designed with your students. (In Steps 5, 6, and 7, we offer guidance on how to fully implement this design—collecting data, analyzing it, and bringing your findings back to bear on the curriculum.) For example, short empirical research experiments can help students engage with the New Deal in at least four distinct ways:

1. Understand the *legacy or continuing impact* of the New Deal reform era or individual New Deal programs or legislation.
   - *Short Experiment*: If possible, have students visit a local New Deal Works Progress Administration (WPA) mural and undertake a short (30-minute) participant observation exercise to understand how people today engage with these murals.
2. Understand *contemporary attitudes* about the New Deal as a reform movement or as specific federal programs or legislation.
   - *Short Experiment*: Develop a short three-question True or False survey that asks adults in the students' family network about their attitudes toward the New Deal. One question might ask: True or False: The New Deal was an example of American socialism?
3. Assess *current knowledge* of the New Deal or a particular New Deal program.
   - *Short Experiment*: Have each student conduct a short three-question interview about the New Deal with two registered voters. One question might ask: Do you know when and under what circumstances Social Security was created?
4. Explore the ethical *dimensions* of the New Deal.
   - *Short Experiment*: In class exercise: Was the (first) Agricultural Adjustment Act (AAA) good government policy in 1933?
     - » You are tenant farmer in North Carolina.
     - » You are an animal rights advocate.
     - » You are the Secretary of the Department of Agriculture.

Ideas for designing short empirical experiments in or out of class.

- It is best to think of these empirical experiments as a *substitute for a traditional research paper that offers a different kind of stretch and introduces new skills and mindsets.* Just as a research paper will require both in-class time to introduce as well as to explain the assignment and out-of-class time to complete the assignment, so too will these experiments.

- To bypass the work of contacting people in your community, we suggest *using methods that do not require elaborate coordination and logistics. Methods that students can undertake themselves after short instruction:* short surveys or interviews are best with peers, school staff, family members, acquaintances, or people in the family networks of your students. Whenever possible, bring respondents to your school.
- For every topic, focus on *identifying relevant people or organizations that you know, other teachers know, or that are part of social networks of your students and their families*—it is easier and less time-consuming to ask someone you know to respond to a request for an interview.
- Increase the number of respondents by *creating teams of two students and having each team collect data.*
- *Keep it short*—interviews and survey with three questions are perfectly fine for a short curricular experiment; they take up less of the respondent's time and are easier to analyze.

Resource

Here is an outline that illustrates how to sequence field research for semester or yearlong research projects. We use the research question introduced in the case study as an example: *How do leaders in sustainability and climate change in our country move people from concern to action?*

Phase 1: What did our conversations with other researchers teach us about what and how we should design our field research to answer a research question?

- What methods might be best to use?
- The benefits and challenges of surveys, interviews, and focus groups for our question.
- The need to consider how our data will be processed after it is collected.

Is there consensus that one method—say, in-depth interviews—are the most effective method to use to understand how leaders of government offices and NGOs working in the area of sustainability get people to move from concern to action. Or is there no consensus and thus room to try a new method?

- What questions have other researchers interested in this question asked their human subjects?
- What did they find, so we can phrase our questions to test these findings?

Phase 2: Teacher planning time is focused on developing lessons that enable students to work through the three research design decisions:

Decision 1: Which people or organizations would most effectively help answer your research question?

Decision 2: Would questioning or observing people be the best way to answer our question?

Decision 3: If questioning people, what method will be most effective?

Phase 3: Students and teachers choose a research method, make a short argument for why this data collection method is the appropriate method to answer the research question, and develop effective research tools and questions/prompts.

Phase 4: Students test/pilot their survey, focus group prompts, and or interview questions with peers and or family members and revise based on the feedback they receive.

TEACHING

Over the years, we and the teachers we have worked with have developed a cluster of insights that can help teachers design empirical research in which you and your students collect new data.

First, the biggest challenge in this step is accurately assessing how much time empirical research will take. There are two basic insights that are relevant: (1) precisely because this involves humans, social science research always takes longer than you think it will; and (2) the only way you can accurately gauge how long a research step will take for you will be to do it *and* keep a record of how long it takes for future reference. We have found that if a teacher underestimates the time involved, the research experience will be rushed or incomplete, making it less satisfying for students. So initially, be conservative, take on less, even if you think you can do more. What does conservative research design look like? Here are some suggestions:

- If possible, interview people you and your students have immediate access to, because the logistics of arranging interview times and identifying interview locations are extremely time-consuming. Consider interviewing class members, someone in the school, the student's immediate network, or family friends.
- For short curricular experiments, first consider if a question can be answered or concept tested by student observation because students can do this on their own and do not need to wait for logistical details to be completed—such as coordinating schedules for interviews.

- If you and your students don't have time to pilot focus group prompts with people, troubleshoot them yourself and then use them and learn.
- A two-question interview and a single focus group can produce new knowledge.

Second, don't lose sight of the essential thinking and doing of this step. For short curricular-based experiments, the goal is to have students *experience* how to "test" concepts by making their own observations and asking questions of people. For semester or yearlong research community projects, the goal is for students to start making and explaining their own empirical research design decisions. Everything else—the length of the survey, even the data collection method that is chosen—is secondary. Everything else is secondary, because students can get better at these skills by practicing them later. They cannot, however, properly grasp what is involved unless they first try playing the research game.

ASSESSMENT

Formative Assessment

Self-Assessment. After making research design decision #1, have students use a 3×5-inch index card (or its digital equivalent) to respond to one of the following prompts designed to assess research progress thus far:

- Is there anything *you* could do next time to be better informed about people and groups in your community?
- What are the most challenging parts of identifying the people or groups our class should speak to in order to answer our research question or test a concept?
- Is there a group that we should survey or interview, but who may not be willing or able to participate? If yes, come up with a strategy that would address their concerns and/or enable them to participate.

Summative Assessment

Quiz. After providing an overview of data collection methods, have students take the following True or False quiz:

_____ Surveys are a great method for understanding people's deepest feelings. (F—in-depth interviews would be best for this.)

_____ The participant observation method is best for research questions that involve understanding what people actually do, not what they say they will do. (T)

_____ If you are doing a focus group, you should be concerned about strong personalities dominating the conversation. (T)

_____ The in-depth interview method would be best if you were interested in the detailed experiences of 4–5 people? (T)

Bonus: Develop a research question that would be a good fit for the focus group method: _____

Performance Tasks

Individual Performance Task. After reviewing the strengths and weaknesses of the four primary research methods, have students:

a. Select the most effective method to answer their research question or test a concept.

b. Develop a paragraph rationale that convinces others that they have made the best choice.

These choices and rationales could be presented in the form of a 30-second presentation or a bulleted one-page list presented to the class or a panel of peers, teachers, or community members.

Group Performance Tasks. *Create an effective research tool.* Have research teams:

a. Develop a first draft of a survey, focus group prompts, in-depth interview, and so on.

b. Pilot the tool on family members or classmates.

c. Revise tool based on input received from the pilot.

d. Use the tool to collect data in the community, noting any issues with the tool in the process of data collection.

e. Submit final tool and data for grade.

FREQUENTLY ASKED QUESTIONS

Q: How do you know if you have chosen the right method to test a concept or answer the research question?

A: The nature of research is such that you can't know definitively. What you can do is:

1. Look at how other researchers have designed research that tries to answer an analogous question or test a hypothesis similar to yours.

2. Understand the benefits and weaknesses of each method.

3. Assess the tradeoffs of each method—such as the survey method provides many responses, but limits the range and nature of the responses. Is that a good fit for your question?
4. Make a case for why the method chosen is the best method to answer the question.
5. Try the method and see what you learn and incorporate that into your design work next time.

Remember, research is always about two kinds of learning. The first kind of learning is what you and your students discover from previous researchers and what you and your students understand from doing research in a self-aware, conscious manner. The second type of learning is what we learn from mistakes. Even if you and your students select an ineffective method for your question, if you come to understand why the fit was bad and make better design decisions the next time, that is a net positive. Think of the baseball pitcher who loses the game because the opposing batter realized he only trusted his fastball, waited for that pitch, and hit a home run. If this loss convinces him to work on his curve, the experience was valuable.

Thinking and Doing the TfC Method Is Intended to Develop Lifetime Researchers

Q: How do you know you have an effective survey or interview question or focus group prompt?

A: The best questions/prompts are those that make it easy for people to be honest as they provide responses that are relevant. This is true even or especially when responses are unexpected *and can* be easily analyzed by you and your students. We have found it helpful to brainstorm the range of responses that we believe a question will illicit and then provide answer options for the most common of these responses. We urge you to pilot the survey questions or focus group prompts to check both the tone and substance of the questions/prompts. Finally, you should revise as needed—for example, "We now realize a prompt with the phrase 'Second Amendment' will inhibit some of our respondents, so let's rephrase."

In regard to analyzing the results, we urge teachers and students to skim Step 6 and visualize what the data will look like when collected. For example, when students see what 200 survey responses look like on a spreadsheet, they realize why it is not a good idea to have open-ended—fill-in-the-blank or "other"—answer options unless absolutely necessary because they are so hard and time-consuming to analyze.

Q: Isn't it presumptuous to say that students simply by making observations or questioning people can bring *knowledge* to bear on the curriculum or a community problem?

A: No. All knowledge comes from a process similar to that which we encourage you and your students to undertake in this step:

1. Posing a question and perhaps advancing a hypothesis.
2. Answering and/or testing this hypothesis by making observations and asking questions in the world.
3. Analyzing the data obtained to identify key findings that can yield new information.

This is not at all inconsistent with being honest about the limited nature of the experiments you and your students will undertake and the extent of the data that this new knowledge is based on. Of course, it is important to resist the temptation to overstate what you and your students have done. *TfC* students simply state what they have done and use language that is modest in tone—for example, "because of its limited nature, our research findings are, of course, suggestive and preliminary."

eTOOLBOX: RESOURCES

A range of resources for this step—including, hints, activities, lecture outlines, and samples of student work—may be found on the resource page of the *TfC* website: https://www.tools4changeseminar.com/resources.html

Data

Researching with Integrity: Ethical Data Collection

The heart of the *TfC* research method involves collecting data from human subjects to answer a research question. Field research is most productive if participants trust you and your students. Trust is more likely if research participants believe they are being treated with respect and the research process is being undertaken with integrity.

When data collection is undertaken in the classroom, among peers, or between a student and extended family members, a level of trust already exists and student researchers can easily reinforce and build on this trust. However, when data is collected outside the school, in the community and with people who do not know your students, this trust must be established from the ground up. In these cases—especially in these cases—your students must demonstrate by their words and actions that they are deserving of the trust of research participants and the community.

Your students can build this trust by collecting data in an ethical manner. This *TfC* step helps you do this. Specifically, this step guides you through the process of obtaining informed consent from potential participants, teaches you how to respectfully interact with research participants, and demonstrates how to record these interactions.

CASE STUDY

The case study that follows is the Methods and Data Collection section of a *TfC* research report. The question that this report was designed to answer was: *Why do adults in the Town of Rye, New York, lack basic information about the voting process, issues, and candidates?* (Note some of the students who took the lead in writing this section had previous experience with *TfC*.)

Methods and Data Collection

As in every step in our research, we were focused on understanding and improving the voting experiences of people in our community. We decided to use a two-step design to answer this research question. First, we created a survey to

71

get a general sense of how informed people felt they were about voting logistics and issues, where they got their information, and how satisfied they were with this information. Second, we conducted two focus groups that complemented the general picture the survey produced with more in-depth and personal views of the challenge of being a well-informed voter. Together, the survey and the focus groups gave us an answer to our research question.

Survey. The survey itself contained 14 questions and was designed to be administered to both voters and nonvoters. The questions were designed to collect demographic data as well as learn about the kinds of information that adults were getting about candidates, the issues they represented, as well as the sources of this information. For this survey, we decided to begin with a few demographic questions. We role-played the survey collection process, we timed how long it would take for busy people to take it, and then we went to the Kohl's Shopping Plaza in Port Chester, New York, to administer the survey. All 14 questions could be answered in less than 3 minutes—including greeting and thanking everyone who stopped to take it.

Administering Our Survey. On a winter Sunday, from 10:00 A.M. to 12:00 P.M., three volunteer students from our class went out with pens, clipboards, and surveys in both English and Spanish to Kohl's Shopping Plaza. One student also gave out surveys at Blind Brook High School to seniors who were of voting age and teachers who live in the Town of Rye. While we did not have the resources to get a random sample that represented the Town of Rye, we decided that Kohl's Shopping Plaza would be a good place to administer most surveys because, we reasoned, there might be a large potential group of survey candidates shopping on a Sunday morning.

Focus Groups. We conducted two focus groups to gain an understanding of the deeper sentiments that adult residents of the Town of Rye might have if they were engaged in a focused discussion on voting. The main goal of our focus group was to gain an understanding of the meaning behind the survey results. The focus groups were primarily made up of friends and family. We recruited them by telling them about our project and simply asking them to help us by participating. We recognized that this method of recruitment would create the possibility of bias within our focus groups.

Conducting Our Focus Group. The following script was used to welcome participants and lay out common ground rules to facilitate discussion:

"Welcome everyone. We so much appreciate your willingness to share your experience voting in local, state, and federal elections. Feel free to contribute as much or as little as you feel comfortable, but we do hope you speak up. Please respect others in the group, as this is a discussion, not a debate. Remember that although we will be recording this session, we will not make public any identifying information."

Here are the primary prompts we used to elicit comments and direct the conversation toward our research question:

- What comes to mind when you hear stories of low voter turnout?
- Who or what influences your voting tendencies?
- How do you educate yourselves on the issues?
- Why aren't people more aware of issues, candidate positions, and the voting process?

KEY FEATURES

Researchers are expected to act in accordance with ethical obligations. These obligations are duties that come with being a researcher. These obligations are like the values that are instilled in us by our parents and that we live by. That is, they are nonnegotiable duties that go with being a family member or, in this case, with being a member of the research community. Because students will encounter binding codes of conduct when they sign a college honor code or enter any profession, it is extremely helpful for them to begin to understand that ethical conduct is often not chosen, but is instead an obligation that is freely assumed.

The *TfC* method seeks to highlight the ethical dimensions of research to grow better researchers and citizens. In Step 1, we provided guidance to help students reason *ethically* and to bring an *ethical perspective* to bear on their curriculum and/or challenges in their community. In Steps 3 and 4, we introduced the idea that all researchers, including your students, have an ethical obligation to be honest and trustworthy both in regard to how they characterize and present the work of others and how they design their own research. In this step—precisely because it involves the human subjects that are the focus of data collection efforts—we extend and broaden the discussion of ethical behavior. Indeed, the most important ethical obligation is centered on how researchers treat the people who participate in their research.

Informed Consent

Ensuring that research participants agree to participate in the research you and your students are conducting in a free and informed manner is the ethical foundation of data collection involving human subjects. Informed consent requires that potential participants are told about the nature of the research, that participation is always voluntary, and that the benefits and, most importantly, any risks associated with participation are made clear. Consent can take many forms, depending on the participants involved and the risks associated with the research. In the planning section, we clarify what forms of consent are required in each research undertaking. In all cases, researchers are expected to be respectful of the dignity and rights of people who engage in the research process.[1]

Managing the Data Collection Process with Integrity

In the *TfC* method, research integrity extends to all aspects of the relationship with research participants. The human subjects who participate in students' research are not simply another source of information, like an historical document, a fossil, or a webpage. Moreover, research participants are doing you and your students a huge favor by taking your survey or agreeing to be interviewed.

PLANNING

This planning section is written to help you and your students carry out research in an ethical manner, whether your students are interviewing relatives as part of very brief curricular-based experiment or surveying hundreds of community members as part of a semester or yearlong *TfC* action research project. While the ethical obligations are similar in both instances, the way these obligations will be satisfied will vary depending on the research and the relationship between researcher and participant.

Ethical data collection requires that you and your students treat research participants with respect and the data they provide with care. Students learn to act in a respectful manner toward research participants by first recalling and applying what they have learned at home, by examining models of how other researchers—including students like themselves—have met specific ethical obligations, such as obtaining informed consent, and by watching how their teachers interact with research participants.

One Mindset, Three Planning Tasks

Here, we introduce an ethical researching mindset and discuss how this mindset informs the three planning tasks in this step:

1. Obtaining informed consent from research participants.
2. Ensuring respectful and gracious relationships with research participants.
3. Managing the logistics of data collection and preserving a record of data collection.

Developing an Ethical Research Mindset. It is easy for researchers, especially young researchers, to view the person they are interviewing as only a means to

an end—that is, as a source of information. Moreover, because research, especially when it is undertaken in the community, can be time-consuming, it will
be tempting for your students to understand that extracting this information as
efficiently as possible is their primary job. However understandable this may be,
this approach invariably yields poor data. If research participants are seen only as
a means—"yet one more interview"—then it is unlikely that your students will
treat these participants with the dignity, respect, and courtesy they deserve as
human beings and that your students would want for themselves. For example,
we want students to be sensitive enough to notice if a focus group participant
becomes uncomfortable when a discussion takes an unexpectedly personal turn.

Ethical codes have been developed to help researchers treat their participants with respect. Codes of ethics spell out the duties of a researcher and provide
principles that can guide the actions of researchers throughout the inquiry process. Consistently following an ethical code of conduct is also the most effective
way to build trust with your research participants as well as other researchers and
those who will read and use your findings.

In regard to data collection involving human subjects, ethical research codes
are straight forward: Researchers are required to act with integrity. They are expected to be honest, fair, and respectful, especially with people who might participate in their research. In everything they do, they seek to inspire trust and
confidence. This integrity begins with the process by which you and your students
provide information so that people can freely and in an informed manner decide
to participate in the research. It continues throughout the research process and
culminates in ensuring that research participants have access to (and own) the
data they have provided to you and your students.

We encourage you and your students to develop your own research code of
ethics for your data collection work and hold students accountable for living up
to it. The best place to begin drafting a code of ethics is with common sense: If
you (or your students) were asked to participate in a research project, how would
you like to be treated? Then, you and your students should look at examples of
research codes of ethics, both those drafted by professional organizations[2] and by
other *TfC* students. There is no one correct code of research ethics. A code of ethics can be simple or complex. What is important is that students understand that
they have an obligation—that is a duty—to follow the code of ethics they have
developed. This duty is not optional; it comes with the job of being a researcher.

Resource

This is a code of ethics that a group of Duke students at the Kenan Institute for
Ethics developed for a research project called "Uprooted/Rerouted," which they
did with the participation of refugees in Jordan. They reduced this to a lami-
nated, wallet-size card so they could carry it into the field with them as they did
their interviews in a large refugee camp in Jordan. This code of ethics is far more

elaborate[3] than anything you will need in your school, but it gives you an idea of what research ethics might entail. We want to emphasize how the Duke students made this code of ethics their own. It is written with an understanding of what ethical standards would be most challenging for *their* group to uphold. Finally, it is important to note that they chose to use language that was not overly formal or technical.

(On the front of a laminated, wallet card.)
Uprooted/Rerouted Code of Ethics
- Obtain informed consent
- Do not harm people's safety and dignity
- Prioritize people over knowledge acquisition
- Maintain privacy and confidentiality
- Stick to the truth
- Limit personal desires or goals
- Let the research stand for itself
- Cite everything
- Understand the effects of dissemination
- Acknowledge positionality and omissions
- Disclose methods and biases

(On the back of the card.)
Compiled and adopted from Code of Ethics of the American Association of Anthropologists, Association of Social Science Researchers, and American Political Science Association.
    By: (list of students on research team)

Planning Task One: Obtaining Informed Consent

As new researchers, it is tempting to believe there is one correct way to obtain informed consent from potential participants and this involves legal documents and maybe even lawyers. That is not the case.

There is no "right" procedure[4] or "correct" words you must say to obtain informed consent. The best way to approach informed consent is to again imagine what information you would want to know before you would agree (or allow your child) to fill out a survey or participate in a focus group. Before any of us would freely consent to participate in research, we would, surely, want to be free of any form of coercion and be informed:

a. About the point of the research.
b. About what participation does and does not involve.
c. Of any downside associated with participation.
d. Of what happens to the data that is provided.

This is the basic information that you and your students should provide to your research subjects so that they may freely and in an informed manner consent to participate in your research.

Here is a detailed discussion of this basic information and how to communicate it.

Explaining the Purpose of Community Research. Informed consent requires that researchers are honest about the purposes of their research. While researchers may never lie, or withhold information necessary for a participant to make an informed decision, it is necessary to provide honest information about the nature of the research in a manner that does not bias potential participants. For example, when a *TfC* class was examining how lowering the minimum voting age to 16 might impact the behavior of registered voters, they did not want to unduly influence people who would be taking the survey by mentioning 16-year-old voters—an issue the class knew elicited strong opinions among adults in the town. So, the students told potential survey takers the survey was designed to "understand how changes in who is eligible to vote might impact citizenship."

Explaining What Participation Involves. People cannot make an informed decision about whether they want to participate in your research unless they know how long it will take to complete a survey, interview, or what is involved in focus group participation. This includes making it clear that no one is required to participate and that they are free to decline to answer any of the questions and may end their participation in the research at any time.

Explaining Any Risks to Participation. *TfC* research has never asked questions that would put our participants at any risk,[5] and we strongly urge you not to ask such questions. We also never ask questions that would make a person uncomfortable. We never collect any identifiers that would allow someone outside the research team to connect people to individual responses. (For, example, names, addresses, phone numbers, or—in cases where the number of participants is so small that individual identities could be surmised—race, age, and gender.) This ensures that responses will be confidential. If you and your students do not ask sensitive questions and do not keep identifiers, there is little if any downside to people participating in your research. Regardless of the risk involved, if you want to include people under 18 years of age in your research, a parent, guardian, and/ or school official should be contacted. Because of the lack of risk involved in *TfC* research and its educational benefits, parental permission is rarely if ever refused.

Explaining What Happens to the Data. Today, researchers are rethinking traditional notions of "community involvement." Increasingly, it is understood that community involvement goes beyond providing data and includes access to and ownership of the data community members have provided. This is especially relevant when researchers come into a community, collect data, and then depart. This is less of an issue when you and your students are part of the community. However, we would recommend that you make it clear that you and your students will be happy to provide a copy of the final report or presentation and, in the case of surveys, a summary of survey results.

Ways of Obtaining Informed Consent. There are many ways the above information can be communicated and informed consent obtained. For most research that carries no risks to participants, you can provide this information orally. For most online surveys, informed consent can be attained at the beginning of the survey with a statement explaining the research and how it is conducted and then asking the reader to continue to the first survey question. What is critical is that basic information is communicated clearly and you and your students do not apply any pressure on people to participate in your research.

Here are some examples of how *TfC* students obtained informed consent:

1. *Verbal consent. TfC* students asked perspective participants the following question to obtain consent for a two-question interview for a brief social studies experiment.

   "In my history class, we are asking people about the impact of the Great Depression on their lives. Would you be willing to answer my two-question survey?"

2. *Implied consent. TfC* students drafted the paragraph in the resource that follows to provide the basic information a person would need to have in order to make an informed decision about participating in their research. It appeared on the first page of an online survey. If the person went on to complete the survey, it could be assumed they had consented.

Resource

"The following is a confidential survey designed by students in a Tools for Change social science research seminar. The purpose of this survey is to understand the transition to life after high school. The survey will take less than 10 minutes to complete. All responses are confidential. To ensure the validity of this study, we ask that you only provide answers that reflect your views. Do you agree to provide answers that reflect your own views?"

3. *Written consent.* Written consent is essential when minors will participate in the research.

Resource

This is a letter asking parents/guardians to allow their high school student to participate in a *TfC* focus group:

Dear Parents/Guardians:

Your student is participating in the Tools for Change, community research project. Under our supervision, the Tools for Change students will be conducting focus groups made up of younger members of our program. These focus groups will examine how families influence youth in their communities. Your child is invited to participate in the focus group.

Your child's participation in the focus group is voluntary. Juniors and seniors from the Tools for Change class will lead the discussion, take written notes, and audiotape the session to help them write about what they have learned. What your child says during the focus group is confidential. His/her real name will not be included in any reports written about the focus group. The only people who will have access to the notes, audiotape recordings, or information from the focus group are the Tools for Change students and instructors.

Your child needs your permission to participate in this discussion. We will notify your child about what room to report to via email.

Please complete the attached permission slip and have your child bring it to the Tools for Change class by XXX. If you have questions or concerns about this focus group, please do not hesitate to contact: XXX

Thank you in advance for your support on this project.

Permission Form for Parents/Guardians—Tools for Change Focus Group

(Insert date)

My child, _____

(Please print your child's name clearly)

- may participate in the focus group.
- may NOT participate in the focus group.

I understand that my child will participate during his/her regular class period.

_____

Parent/Guardian

Planning Task Two: Ensuring Respectful and Even Gracious Interactions with Research Participants

It is all too easy to forget that the people who agree to complete a survey, consent to be interviewed, or participate in a focus group are doing you and your students a huge favor. They are giving you their time to help your class. More than that, they have agreed to focus their attention on an issue they may not care about and certainly do not care about to the degree that you and your students might. We tell our students that a research participant is best thought of as someone who is going out of their way to bring us a gift. And in response to this act of kindness, we should be unfailingly appreciative, gracious, and solicitous.

Communicating with Research Participants. All correspondence, formal and informal, oral and written, should convey a desire to make participation as easy as possible for research subjects. This is true of brief curricular-based interviews with people your students know as well as in more involved research projects. While it is true that you and your students are working within the rigid structure of the school day, there are still many ways to be accommodating and solicitous of your research participants. For example, interviews may be conducted by trained student pairs after school and over the phone. If at all possible, you should try to offer participants at least two and ideally three interview times.

Most teachers, of course, simply have limited degrees of freedom in regard to scheduling. We have found that the most effective communication is honest about this fact and recognizes that this may, of course, make it more difficult for an interested adult to participate in your research. A teacher struck the right note in an email that concluded: "Unfortunately, our school schedule only permits two windows for the focus group we discussed. Please forgive us for offering just two options. We know you are incredibly busy and wondered if there is any chance you could make one of those times work? Thank you for considering this request." The key here is to be as flexible as possible, regret that you cannot be more flexible, and be genuinely appreciative when research participants accommodate your schedule. It is essential that students see and thus learn how to respectfully and courteously interact with research subjects who have decided to help them with their research. Beyond the immediate requirements of your research, this is a style of engaging with community members that we want our students to learn as citizens.

Resource

Here is a letter that *TfC* students and their teacher wrote asking climate change and sustainability leaders in their county if they might be willing to be interviewed.

Dear XXX,

We are members of Tools for Change, an action-research project that brings together students from area high schools to work on community challenges such as civic participation, youth employment, and hunger in the community. This year, Tools for Change is focused on sustainability in Westchester County. As a community climate leader, we want to interview you as part of our investigation into why it is so challenging to move citizens from every demographic from concern to action despite the overwhelming evidence that doing so is necessary for a sustainable future.

To help us explore the reasons behind this issue, we are interviewing leaders who work in the area of sustainability and climate change to get insight into how people move from concern to action on sustainability issues.

We know you are very busy and would appreciate any time you might give us to discuss your perspectives on this issue. We can generally meet after 4:00 on Wednesdays and Fridays and are willing to travel to meet you at your convenience.

You can contact me/us at this phone number:

Thank you for your consideration.

Sincerely,

Interviews and Focus Groups. When a research participant agrees to come to your school, your students should be prepared to be cordial hosts from the time they arrive. "Do they need a bottle of water?" "Is someone speaking with them or are they standing uncomfortably by themselves?" "Do they need a quick tour of the school?" One *TfC* class invented the role of "focus group managers," assigned students to this role, and entrusted them with the responsibility of ensuring that participants were at ease and comfortable from the time that they entered the school building until they departed.

It is best to think of the interview or focus group as a respectful, attentive conversation rather than an interrogation aimed at extracting information. If research participants sense that the researcher is not treating the interview process with respect, they are less likely to make the effort to honestly and thoughtfully respond to questions. Student interviewers and focus group facilitators need to practice being attentive and engaged. This requires that your students are mentally engaged and that their body language conveys this engagement. Therefore, we suggest you have students practice conducting interviews and facilitating focus groups with other students before doing so with community members.

Attention and engagement will also allow your students to hear the unexpected comments that provide breakthrough research insights. When a student hears something unexpected in an interview, they need to decide immediately if this is a surprising comment that will help answer the research question and thus requires an impromptu follow-up question. Students simply can't make these quick decisions if they are not paying attention.

If your class is conducting interviews or focus groups, consider which of your students are attentive, respectful, empathetic, and/or good with people. These students should be doing the interviewing, leading focus groups, or approaching people to take a survey, and so on. Remember, these traits often have little or nothing to do with grades.

Resource

Interview Protocol. This protocol was produced by a *TfC* class to be used by student teams conducting in-depth interviews with climate change and sustainability leaders.

Notes to interviewers:
- Look carefully at the website of the organization or government office *before* your interview.
- Remember to be respectful and, above all, listen.

Opening Script. "Thanks for taking the time to speak with us. I am a member of Tools for Change, an action-research project that brings students together from area high schools to address a community challenge. This year, we are focused on sustainability and how to move people from concern about this issue to action. We are interviewing Westchester County leaders, such as yourself, and we will circle back to you with our findings."

Questions:
1. What are your greatest challenges working in the areas of sustainability and/or climate change?
2. Why do you do what you do? What or who has inspired you to act on these issues?
3. How do you get volunteers/citizens/students to get involved in this work?
     Possible follow-up questions:
     » Why do people volunteer?
     » What qualities are you looking for?
     » What has worked in regard to attracting volunteers/citizens/ students?
     » What has not worked?
4. How do you (or your organization) move people from awareness to action in regard to sustainability?
     Possible follow-ups:
     » How important is passion and is giving money an "action"?
     » Do your strategies differ depending on age, race, and gender?
5. What else should I know about moving from people from concern to action, but did not ask?
6. Who else should we be talking to about these issues?

Resource: "Focus Group 101":

Student Guide for Planning and Conducting a Focus Group

1. Develop and type a script to be read to get informed consent. The script should include:

- The issue under investigation.
- The research question (in simple terms).
- Who is doing the study.

- Who will see the completed study.
- How long the interview will take.
- How we will assure confidentiality through anonymity.
- How we will refer to participants as an assigned number during the interview. Place cards or give out name tags with each person's assigned number.
- Notification if the interview is taped and will result in a transcript.
- Assurance from students that focus group participants' responses will not be distributed and that notes and audio will not be shared with anyone beyond the research group.
- Participants can be given numbers and referred to by their numbers for the sake of privacy if there is any question about the use of their names.

2. Roles. Wisely choose—or have student themselves choose in a secret ballot—the students who will play the following roles: (1) focus group managers: overall quality control; (2) moderator (facilitator) of the focus group; (3) note taker or audio recorder. The remaining students serve as "observing researchers" and are responsible for observing, taking notes during the interview, and asking follow-up questions (see below).

3. Note taking. Note-takers should type prompts/questions and leave room on paper under each prompt/question for notes on participant answers. The focus group moderator should use a hardcopy and handwrite any notes they take—such as key comments, and so on. This way, during the conversation, it is easier to follow up planned prompts with spontaneous questions. The reason that the moderators should take notes with paper and pen is because typing into a laptop or tablet interferes with the interviewer's eye contact and that should be maintained with members of the group. More complete sets of notes will be made by student observers whose typing won't interfere with the rapport necessary for a successful focus group experience. Copy the informed consent script and distribute to all participants. Then read it aloud.

Even if the observing students are fast typists or write quickly, it is easy to miss parts of the conversation when the interview is in progress. We have found it is best when students decide ahead of time what kind of shorthand they should use while recording answers during a focus group discussion. A shared shorthand style means notes can be shared and understood during data analysis. For example:

- F1 and P1 might mean Focus Group 1 and Participant 1.
- Or, use F1 and the initial or number of participants.

4. Organize room. Move chairs into a circle with the participants sitting next to one another or seat everyone around a table, making sure that everyone can see one another. Then, depending on the topic or level of confidentiality that is appropriate, either distribute the number tags to participants or have a trifold stand-up identifying nameplate with each focus group participant's first name.

- Remember: Moderators who are running the group only take simple handwritten notes and record follow-up ideas for new questions—all other researchers take extensive notes and may use laptops or notepads.
- After each moderator asks a question and participants answer, the floor can be opened to the observing researchers to see if someone wants to add a follow-up question. The moderator may want to ask follow-ups as well.
- The teacher should only interrupt if the follow-ups are too leading or if a vital issue or question is missing or unclear.

Planning Task Three: Managing the Logistics of Data Collection and Preserving a Record of Your Work

Data collection involves coordinating the movement of your students and adults with busy professional lives, so it is best to invest time in planning at the outset. Research is nothing if not humbling. Even with the best laid plans, the unexpected can and will happen. For example, people sometimes do not show up for a focus group even when they have agreed to come and have been reminded numerous times through a variety of media. Flexibility and adaptability are necessary in all aspects of research; they are especially important in the data collection stage.

Circumstances and Constraints. A recurring theme in this guide is the importance of being honest about your circumstances and constraints and planning research accordingly. We have consistently recommended that you be conservative in planning your first research experiences, if only to ensure the experience is positive for you and your students. In regard to data collection, don't put undue pressure on yourself or your students by believing that data is worthless unless you have a statistically significant sample. We tell our students and ourselves that no one has perfect data. At the university level, a statistically significant sample costs money and is often paid for with a grant. At the high school level, there is no grant money or research funding so you should do the best you can and then let your audience know that you recognize the limits of your data.

Some *TfC* classes have held a single focus group. Other *TfC* classes received 30–40 completed surveys because that was what was possible. In their reports and presentations, students were honest about why they had only one focus group and then adapted a humble and modest tone when discussing their findings. On the other hand, some *TfC* classes were able to obtain a representative sample for their surveys. Valerie tells her students that they should have at least three interviews to triangulate data and at least 25 surveys to gain a reasonable understanding of what participants or respondents are sharing with the research team. With these goals in mind, she has found that students like to go above and beyond these small benchmarks. In many cases, students have prided themselves on gathering hundreds of surveys and have conducted multiple focus groups, so don't underestimate your students. Again, the point of *TfC* is to have your students play the research game.

All Students Love the Data Collection Step

Even when you have been honest about what your capacity is, the logistics of data collection can present challenges. While we provide resources on our website, the best learning is by doing. For example, TfC students in Westchester County, New York, and Newark, New Jersey, were confident they could get high school students to take their online survey about the transition from high school to college. They tried a variety of strategies. The least successful strategy involved "just asking friends." What the students learned was that they didn't feel comfortable "pressuring" friends to take their survey, they didn't want to "use up" a favor by asking a friend to take the survey, and/or they couldn't convince friends that taking a survey could lead to positive change. The most successful strategies involved going directly to teachers—for example all the freshmen English teachers—explaining the importance of the survey and asking if they would post the link and encourage students in all of their classes to take the survey in the first 2 minutes of class.

Looking Ahead. Once people have agreed to take your survey, sit for an interview, or participate in focus group discussions, it is critical to have a record of your survey results or an accurate transcript of interviews and focus group discussions. It will be most helpful if you and your students collect, organize, and display your data in a way that makes it easy for you to analyze it. Online surveys—Google Forms or Survey Monkey—provide survey results free of charge and in a variety of formats. Most *TfC* students have recorded interviews and then transcribed them. The usual practice with focus groups is to assign two or more students to take notes independently using abbreviations.

Keeping a Record. Finally, for a semester or yearlong research project, you and your students will want to keep a narrative of your data collection process and a record of the decisions you made. This record can be the basis for the "Method and Data Collection" section of a research report or presentation, like the one in the case study in this step. Keeping such a record and producing a data collection section of a report or presentation will make it easier for people to trust the findings and conclusions you and your students develop from your data. This trust will, in turn, make it more likely they will be open to listening to recommendations that you and your students make in regard to addressing a school or community problem.

Specific items your students might want to have notes on:
- Why you choose the method you did
- How you obtained informed consent
- Where and when you collected your data
- What your survey/interview/focus group questions and prompts were
- Count of: interviews, focus groups, focus group participants, completed surveys, and so on

TEACHING

The teaching challenge in this step involves stretching to teach very different skills—from modeling respectful relationships to managing the details of data collection. Over the years, we and the teachers we have been lucky enough to work with have developed a cluster of teaching ideas to help you do this stretching, especially in regard to semester or yearlong research projects.

First, while students can read a research code of ethics and produce their own ethical code, we have found that the behavior of the teacher is the most important factor in determining if classroom research will be conducted ethically. How does the teacher interact with a city council member or social worker who visits the class for an interview? Is the teacher gracious and solicitous? As we write these words, we are deeply aware of both how busy teachers' lives are and the irony of asking even more, but if we believe research and community problem solving is important, this modeling work is as necessary as it is worthwhile.

Second, Bill is not a logical person. Nor is he someone who can think and do sequentially. Instead, he is the father who sets out to empty the trash, but immediately gets distracted and may be found 30 minutes later checking ESPN with the trash overflowing. Valerie, on the other hand, is both logical and sequential as a thinker. But both of us have always found students in our classes who have gifts for managing complex tasks. Identify students who are logically and logistically gifted and support them as they help you manage your data collection.

Third, Bill in his lab at Duke and Valerie in her practice at Rye Neck High School, *never* allow student-written email to go out to school or organizational officials before they read it. Nor do they allow a student to call a community member that the lab or the school has a long-term relationship with before discussing with the student the content and tone of the conversations. College students learn to communicate effectively and respectfully by being mentored. This is even more true of high school students. While this is time-consuming, a single inappropriate email or call can jeopardize an important relationship and your reputation in the community. On the positive side, we have found that the high school students are very quick studies because this kind of communication is clearly something they want to be able to do confidently.

ASSESSMENT

Formative Assessment

Self-Assessment: Journal Entry. Using the actual experience of participating in the administration of a survey, focus group, or interview as background, have students respond to the following prompt:

> "You want to publish a bestselling book on how to conduct a focus group, survey, or interview. Your publisher wants to see your plan for the book before giving you advance money. Specifically, she has asked for the topics you will cover. What are the chapter titles for your proposed book on conducting research?"

Teacher Assessment: Observation and Dialogue. All researchers need to learn to manage the logistics of data collection—such as who, where, when, and how to communicate this information to participants. Students can and should begin to learn to do this logistical planning. The act of planning helps them concretely understand what research involves. Logistical planning is a new skill for most high school students, and teacher guidance is critical. Teacher observation will provide information about whether students understand what research involves on the ground with real people.

Our guidance, then, is best thought of as responding to students' initial thinking by reminding them of steps that they may not have considered and troubleshooting their plans. We have asked our students questions such as: "How will we let people know when and where the focus group will be held?" and "What will you do if most of our participants don't show up?"

- Using the guide "Focus Groups 101" (above) as an example, have student teams develop a list of logistical tasks that need to be completed and the order they need to be accomplished to ensure that data collection runs smoothly.

Summative Assessment

Individual/Group Performances. Using the guide "Focus Group 101" (above) as an assessment standard and after providing opportunities to practice, have groups of students conduct a focus group, survey, or interview. Then, using the copy of the methods section in the case study as a model, write a first draft of your design and methods section, then revise as many times as possible.

We recommend your evaluation be delivered in the form of a conversation with individual students or groups of students. At the completion of the interview/

survey/focus group, *TfC* students have asked participants to share their thoughts on the experience of being part of, for example, a focus group. Feedback from participants can and should be integrated into your evaluation of student work if at all possible.

Making Curricular Connections

The best researchers do not just mechanically complete a set of discrete tasks. They have a style. It is useful to reflect on the research style your students are developing, consciously or unconsciously. Because we have found our students are far more articulate doing oral reflection than written reflection, we have emphasized developing the ability to do written reflections on their research style. Below are some prompts that can be used for short (15-minute) free writing experiences to help develop written reflection:

- What did you learn from conducting research with an individual human subject or group?
- How is conducting research with human subjects different than getting information from people?
- Describe an awkward moment in the data collection process, what you did at the time, and what you could do next time to make it less awkward.
- Must a researcher tell people who might participate in the survey/interview/focus group everything about the research to obtain informed consent?

We have found that many research practices and skills are directly transferable, especially in a community setting. Here are two tasks that provide students with an opportunity to do this work of translation.

- Evaluate, take, and defend a position about requiring informed consent from parents/guardians before asking their opinion on closing a local school.
- Adapt the logistical checklist you created to collect data to create a "get out the vote campaign" in your community.

FREQUENTLY ASKED QUESTIONS

Q. My students are interviewing five friends to understand how the U.S. Constitution impacts youth in their everyday lives as part of an Honors U.S. history class. What do they need to know about research ethics to do these interviews?

A. Before your students conduct their interviews, it is important that they: (1) understand researchers have a duty to treat all research participants—even friends—with respect. This respect entails telling their friends in informal but clear ways why they are interviewing them, informing them of how long it will take, and letting them know that it is not a problem if they do not want to participate, and (2) recognize that their friends are doing them a favor by agreeing to be interviewed and they should convey their appreciation in how they interact with their friends.

Q. How do you know how much information about the research topic needs to be shared with a potential research participant?

A. The basic rule here is to provide sufficient information so that a participant has an accurate sense of the research, while at the same time not needlessly discouraging or biasing people who would otherwise participate. This means you and your students cannot mislead a potential research participant about the subject of your research. If you are studying school violence, you cannot tell a potential research participant that you are studying the grading practices in honors classes because you believe more people will complete a survey on that topic. If you are concerned that the topic of school violence will discourage people from participating, it would be entirely appropriate to state your research interests in language that either captures the broader issues involved or is consistent with how the topic is framed in other research. For example, "our research explores what makes for a healthy, safe, and educational school environment."

eTOOLBOX: RESOURCES

A range of resources for this step—including, hints, activities, lecture outlines, and samples of student work—may be found on the resource page of the *TfC* website: https://www.tools4changeseminar.com/resources.html

Analysis
Analyzing Data to Answer a Research Question

Data doesn't speak for itself. The world is filled with data—interview transcripts, mounds of statistics, and so on. Moreover, the Internet has made data more accessible than ever before. But it is not at all clear that the availability of ever more data has enhanced our ability to address the most pressing problems of our time. The capacity to analyze this data and present findings in an unbiased and persuasive manner will continue to be a critical skill set for our students as they move forward into college and future careers.

More than in any other step in *TfC*, the thinking and doing involved in analyzing data may be found in virtually every list of teaching and learning standards and/or in most social studies curriculum. The exact wording of the standard may change, but here is a common label: "Gathering, Interpreting, and Using Evidence." It is worth remembering that the discrete analytical skills found in state standards were once organic steps in a disciplinary-based method. The *TfC* method is animated by the conviction that these skills are best learned when they are placed back into the methodology from which they emerged and organically made sense. In addition, it is as part of an inquiry method, not as a list of discrete standards, that students will encounter these skills in college and careers.

Teachers, of course, must demonstrate that their students have met state standards. The challenge for *TfC* teachers who want to prepare their students for college and career is to translate the analytical skills and mindsets their students have learned as part of an organic method back into the standards that they and their students are being assessed on. This involves first reminding students that their work in this step is similar to analysis of nonfiction material in other subjects and then helping them to see common analytical skills that are present in all forms of analysis and in state and national standards. In this step, we provide assessments that provide these reminders to students.

In Step 6, we guide you and your students through the process of data analysis. Specifically, this step is intended to help students listen to and analyze data so that they can identify critical themes and patterns that are often hidden in words and numbers. These patterns, in turn, can answer research questions and provide new knowledge that can be brought to bear on the curriculum or community challenges.

CASE STUDY

Here is a lesson that Bill developed to introduce qualitative data analysis to a class of high school students. He began with a question and then helped students sift through a limited amount of data in search of patterns or a key insight that could answer that question. The lesson illustrates how easy it is to give students practice at analyzing data.

Here is how he taught the lesson:

"Today, we are going to look for patterns in data from a list of family expenses."

a. "Since research generally begins with a question, here is the question I want you to answer: What can we learn about the family just from this list of expenses? I will award this bag of M&Ms to the person who provides the most information about this family and supports it with specific evidence from the list of expenses."

b. "Before I give you the list of expenses. I want to talk about what analysis is. I think of analysis as the opposite of magic. It involves a methodical and sequenced process of examination. Here is the method we are going to follow to analyze this data (put on board):

  i. Read through the expenses twice to really get to know the information.

  ii. For each item, make some inferences—educated guesses—about what the item is telling you about the family that owns this account. That is, use the data to make an inference like this: Does the dry-cleaning expense suggest that someone in the family has a job that requires that they wear nice clothes? (Remember: The data can't speak; it can't answer our question on its own. So, you have to do this work.)

  iii. Look for patterns. Create groups or buckets that correspond to these patterns—for example, there are a lot of items that are household expenses; I am going to make a group with that name and put all these items in it.

  iv. Translate the inferences you have made into answers to the question. See how many different answers you can come up with. For example, there is evidence that this family has children because of the many child-related expenses. A pattern emerges once one sees at least three related pieces of evidence; the speech therapy expense along with camp and babysitting expenses support this assumption."

Family Expenses		
Date	Description	Amount
7/10	Speech therapy	$285.00
7/10	N.C. Dept. of Transportation	$33.00
7/11	Dinner out	$95.00
7/11	VISA credit card	$200.00
7/11	Healthy Start Daycare	$1500.00
7/12	Big City Tire Repair	$336.00
7/12	Coffee	$5.00
7/13	Babysitting	$36.00
7/16	Vet visit for Daisy	$49.00
7/17	Grocery Store	$161.35
7/20	Camp	$725.00
7/22	Dry cleaning	$24.75
7/22	Coffee	$5.00
7/23	Grocery Store	$123.44
7/24	Car repair	$365.00
7/30	Student loan	$150.00
8/1	Babysitting	$48.00
8/1	Electric Bill	$135.00
8/1	Mortgage	$1050.00
8/1	Hulu	$56.00
8/1	City: water & sewer	$101.00
8/5	Am Express Credit Card	$400.00
8/6	Dry Cleaning	$33.00

KEY FEATURES

The thinking and doing in this step are twofold:

1. Listening deeply to research participants.
2. Analyzing data to identify patterns that are often hidden across many seemingly different responses.

The goal of data analysis is to discover something that will prompt other researchers to change their minds, force students to think about curricular content differently, or inspire community change. This work of discovery requires a specific kind of listening. This listening can be contrasted with the skills required in Step 1 of the *TfC* method: surfacing one's own perspective as a way of seeing the world. In fact, analyzing data requires that researchers temporarily ignore or put aside their perspective as much as possible. (Being self-conscious of one's own perspective—the focus of Step 1—makes it possible to put it aside.) We can't begin to hear what research participants are saying, or see what they see, if we can't bound our own perspectives. The ability to temporarily put aside our own views does not just happen. It takes a conscious effort. We have to decide to do it. And this work is easier when we are aware of our own values and the tendency to make assumptions about others.

Adam Kahane in his book *Solving Tough Problems* gives us an idea of what this listening looks like. Kahane discusses three kinds of "listening" that he encountered in helping stakeholders from across the social, racial, and political spectrum develop solutions to the biggest challenges facing their nations. In the mid-1990s, South Africa's challenge was to create a new post-apartheid society. The first kind of listening Kahane witnessed in a group of leaders in the new South Africa wasn't listening at all. It was, instead, simply pausing before stating one's views until the previous speaker had finished. This is low-level courtesy, not listening. The second kind of listening was literally hearing what another had said. "I hear the clergy member when he argued for reconciliation at the grassroots level." The third type of listening was what might be called deep listening. It was the ability to *hear and discern* what people in the room were thinking, what existed underneath or within all the words they spoke. Think of this as discerning what the people in the room were trying to say. In the long and difficult conversations in South Africa, what people were trying to convey was that they *recognized* the depth and breadth of the suffering that Black South Africans experienced under apartheid and wanted to seek public ways of acknowledging that reality.

This deep listening is similar to what the best researchers do in analyzing their data. Good researchers are willing and able to discern patterns that are not immediately evident but nevertheless connect dozens or even hundreds of separate pieces of information that come from survey or interview responses. This deep listening informs a well-tested analytical technique, called coding. Coding involves systematically sifting through survey, interview, or focus group data to identify responses that can be grouped together because they share something important in common. Coding enables researchers to distil, sift, and filter hundreds of individual responses into groups that reveal patterns that can then form the answers to research questions.

PLANNING

This section is written to help your students develop the dispositions and skills to analyze all kinds of data. By "all kinds," we mean a range that begins with data you and your students might gather from the Internet, survey data that a sustainability nonprofit has happily given your class in response to your offer to provide free data analysis,[1] and also includes the results from a survey you and your students may have conducted as part of your curriculum and focus group transcripts from a semester or yearlong community research project. There are two essential planning challenges in this step that involve helping your students listen for understanding and develop the analytical skill of coding data to uncover overarching patterns and themes.

Listening with an Open Mind for Understanding

One of the core beliefs of *TfC* is that research can teach students ethical behavior. Learning to adhere to an ethical research code doesn't just teach students to be honest and respectful of research participants; it is also good preparation for an ethical life. Moreover, learning ethics by trying to adhere to a professional code of conduct can sometimes be more effective than a lesson on how to be a good person. Indeed, ethical behavior is, perhaps, best learned when it is intertwined in the way we live and work, not as an abstract topic. The ethical dimension highlighted in this step involves developing the habit of genuinely listening with an open mind in order to understand the views of others. Researchers make the effort to be open mind about opinions of their research subjects and empathetic about ideas that they don't agree with because the point of research is to understand how people think, act, and feel. The best researchers try to get inside the heads of their respondents. When they hear statements they don't agree with or don't understand, they try to put aside their own views and say "Tell me more" and ask themselves, "What would you have to believe to say that?"

We tell our students that data analysis requires a different kind of listening than they usually do. Listening to hear if there are any common interests when choosing a friend or partner, listening to your opponent in a debate, and listening for racist language have little to do with the listening required to analyze data. Indeed, people who are unable or unwilling to *make the effort* to listen with no other motive than to understand simply cannot analyze qualitative data.

Bracketing our own views is hard for all of us. So too is demonstrating the integrity required to listen to people with a range of views and making the effort to understand them. There are very few contemporary situations where students can practice that kind of integrity and be rewarded for developing it. Doing research is one of those rare opportunities.

Here is what this opportunity looks like. A *TfC* class discovered that people could be very upset about the way local government operated and not vote. When the students were discussing this finding, one student described the respondents who did not vote as "lazy." Another student wondered if that was how the respondents would describe themselves? "We told people when we were speaking with them to be honest and that there were no wrong answers," she continued, "now, we can't say that some answers were bad. Maybe," she concluded, "we should describe what our research participants say in words they would recognize themselves as saying."

Resource

A *TfC* class developed this simple checklist that can help you and your students get better at listening to understand:

- Decide that this kind of listening is something you want to be able to do (not all the time, of course, but when the situation calls for it).
- Be aware of your own perspective and values so you can recognize instances when your own views are preventing you from hearing your research subjects.
- Consciously make the effort to temporarily put your own views aside during the data analysis stage.

Data Analysis

Analysis is about identifying underlying patterns or key insights in the data. The most important of these patterns and insights will constitute the (key) findings that can be used to answer your research question. Patterns and insights, however, are not obvious. They don't announce themselves and will not be hiding in plain sight. So, your students can't just copy them down. Instead, your students must methodically uncover these patterns.

While there is no "one" or "right" way to analyze data, your class will want to make sure they proceed in a deliberative manner. "Thinking outside the box" or "winging it" are not effective strategies. Fortunately, there are well-established techniques for teasing out patterns in data. These techniques follow a logical sequence. Here, we lay out techniques for analyzing two kinds of data:

1. Textual responses—such as focus group and interview transcripts and field notes from participant observation that need to be coded.
2. Responses that can be counted—such as survey responses—that can be displayed in tables and graphs.

If you do not already have a favorite coding method for both of these responses, we suggest you try the two slightly different techniques in the resource below and then make revisions or alterations so they work better for you and your students.

Resource

Analyzing Textual Responses—Such as Focus Group and Interview Transcripts.
Begin by appointing two *independent note-takers* to record the work of analysis—such

as what the class did, what the class found, and so on. If you are doing a semester or yearlong research project, these notes can then be the basis for an *Analysis and Findings* section of a report or presentation.

Four-Step Analysis Technique:

1. *Focus your attention* on the question you and your students want to answer. While most data contain all sorts of interesting details, you want your students to concentrate on answering their question. If you are doing a semester or yearlong research project, have your students reread your literature review notes so that they may compare what they find in their data with what other researchers have found. This will help them decide what is interesting or surprising in their data.

2. *Group similar responses.*
   - For interview and focus group transcripts, read through the responses for each focus group prompt/research question at least three times and then *group similar responses*.
   - For each prompt/question, ask students to try to group similar responses or comments; this is called coding. Pick the two groups with the most responses in them and give these groups a name. These group names are called code names. Ideas for code names:
     » The easiest, but *least helpful code names* are simple, generalized descriptions of the responses—such as "responses about being unsafe at night."
     » *The most helpful code names* are phrased as answers to the research question. So, if a question is focused on whether high school students feel safe in their community, one of your coding groups might be named: "Reasons people feel unsafe in the community that are related to the time of day or night."
   - For field notes from participant observation research:
     » Read through field notes two or three times.
     » Develop a list of common themes or topics that reappear in the notes and then group observations under these themes or topics.
   - Mechanics of coding
     » If working with *a hard copy of the interview or focus group transcript or field note,* color-code the sentences that fit under each code name with a different colored pencil or marker.
     » If working with *an electronic version of a transcript or field notes,* cut and paste the statements for each question so they are placed under the group or coding name that best fit them.
     » When you have finished coding the responses or comments for each question or prompt, refocus the attention of your students by asking how these groups can help them answer their research question.

3. After you have coded responses for all your interview questions, focus group prompts, or field notes, identify *overall patterns across all the coding groups* you and your students have made. Some patterns can be eye-balled. For example, one coding group that consistently reappears in several questions/prompts may constitute one overarching pattern. You and your students will *surface* other patterns by coming up with a new more general coding name and placing more specific groups under that general name or by merging one coding group under another group that is similar to the first group or better describes the responses. For example, "comments indicating people feel unsafe at certain times of the day" and "comments indicating people feel unsafe in particular locations" might be combined into a group called: "comments about unsafe locations or times."

4. *Select key findings from your research by identifying coding groups that have many responses and that answer your research question by either: (a) confirming what other researchers have found, (b) bringing to light a surprising finding, or (c) a bit of both.* In general, your key findings should be linked to what most of your respondents have said, or the consensus of the focus group, select coding groups that have many responses grouped under them. Then in a sentence or two, have students explain how these key overall patterns of findings answer the research question. For example, "in our research question [w]e have been interested in why students feel unsafe in the community. One of our key findings is that location and time are the most important factors affecting whether someone feels safe. Being downtown or in county parks at night led most of our research participants to say they felt 'unsafe.'"

Resource

Here is an example of how a *TfC* class coded their focus group responses (note the students merged steps #3 and #4 above.)

Research question: How does family and community impact you?

Prompt to focus group participants (read and have participants complete the sentence):

"I feel my family's influence most in terms of _____.

1. *List all of the responses to this prompt.*
   - How I had to encourage myself to do better.
   - The ways I feel I needed to learn by myself.
   - How dad handles all school work: mom handles shopping and that sort of thing.
   - The ways I feel I needed to teach myself and learn by myself.

- The importance of college because my mom didn't get to go and now I want to be a chef, which she isn't happy about.
- The way my parents are role mentors and encourage me to be independent and do my best.
- The ways that due to caretaking responsibilities for younger siblings, I don't want to have children and want to find my own way.
- The fact that my dad had to walk 10 miles to get to school so he wants me to appreciate the opportunity that I have to do my best.
- My cousin, a mechanic, who opened his own business so that he could be independent.

2. *Code the responses into groups and name the groups.* For example: "Responses that discuss how family influences educational and career goals."
   - The fact that my dad had to walk 10 miles to get to school so he wants me to appreciate the opportunity that I have to do my best.
   - The importance of college because my mom didn't get to go and now I want to be a chef, which she isn't happy about.
   - My cousin, a mechanic, who opened his own business so that he could be independent.

Family (negative and positive) influence on the development of skills—independence and grit:
   - The ways I feel I needed to learn by myself.
   - The way my parents are role mentors and encourage me to be independent and do my best.
   - How I had to encourage myself to do better.

3. *What did we learn from these responses that can help us answer our question?*
   - Most common positive family influences are related to encouraging education and career.
   - Whether the influence of the family was positive or negative, most of the young people developed persistence, independence, and grit as a result of grappling with family influences and their own ideas.

Resource

Analyzing Survey Responses. Begin by appointing two *independent note-takers* to record the work of analysis—such as what the class did, what the class found, and so on. If you are doing a semester or yearlong research project, these notes can then be the basis of an *Analysis and Findings* section for a report or presentation.

Five-Step Analysis Technique:
   1. *Focus your attention on the question you and your students want to answer.* The survey data will contain many interesting details; however, your students should focus on answering their research question. If undertaking a semester or yearlong research report, have your students reread your literature review notes so they may compare what they find in their data

with what other researchers have found. This will help them decide what is interesting or new.

2. *Carefully examine each question and the responses on the charts and graphs of your survey results*. The charts we include here were automatically generated by Google Forms and can also be purchased through Survey Monkey. Ask the following questions (note-takers should record answers):

   • Is this data critical to our research question or is it a background or demographic question?
   • How might we interpret the responses to this question?
     For example, in this survey question: How safe do you feel when you see a police patrol car parked in your neighborhood?

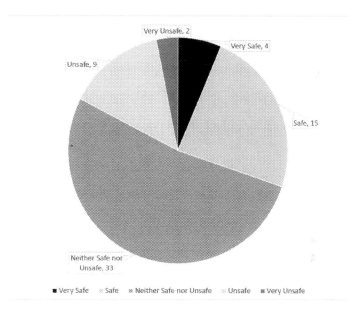

   • Ask students: "What are our respondents telling us in this question?"
   • Then, ask questions that help students formulate answers that:
     » Identify what is essential in the responses and be as precise as possible. For example, "What jumps out at you when you look at the responses?" "Can you summarize how most people felt when they saw a police car?" "You said, 'a lot'; can you be more precise?" A helpful student response to this data would be to note that more than half (33/60) of the students who answered the question felt neither safe nor unsafe when they saw a police car.
   • Ask, does this result:
     » Confirm what we already know?
     » Challenge what we already know?
     » Do a little of both?
     » We don't have enough information to answer this question.

Tell students: "Let's make sure we are focused on what is most important: translate this result into an answer to our research question."

3. *Identify overall patterns that connect many of the responses to the individual survey questions* or an incredibly surprising response to one question. Ask:
   - Does a result from an individual question support, confirm, or help explain results from other questions?
   - If yes, what would you call this pattern?
   - How can this pattern help us answer our research question?

4. *Are there results from individual questions that contradict results from other questions?*
   - If yes, how would you describe this contradiction?
   - Is it possible to reconcile or explain these contradictory results?
   - How can these contradictory findings help us develop a nuanced answer to our research question—for example, "We found that adults believed that high school students would not take full advantage of the opportunity to vote, but still felt high school students should be afforded the right to vote."

5. *Select key findings from your research by identifying overall patterns or coding groups that have many responses and that answer your research question by either (a) confirming what other researchers have found, (b) bringing to light a surprising finding, or (c) a bit of both.* Then, in a sentence or two—that the note-takers can record—explain why these and not other patterns or results are the most important findings from your research. These can then become the key findings from your research and can be used to answer your students' research questions. If you are doing an extended research project, these findings may be featured in the *Analysis and Findings* section of your report or presentation.

TEACHING

Over the years, we and the teachers we have been fortunate to work with have developed a cluster of insights that can help teachers analyze data with their students.

First, as with other research thinking and doing, the best way for students to get better at analyzing data is to analyze data. This is true of any data whether it is derived from a research project, a science experiment, or a historic or literary text. As in other steps in this book, you can't tell your students exactly how to analyze data. You have to show them and then quickly let them try to do it. We suggest you spend some time familiarizing yourself with the steps of the data analysis technique that fits your data, examine some examples of students using this technique on the *TfC* website, develop a plan in which you can briefly model the skill of coding, and give students a chance to do it themselves with your oversight.

Second, there are many ways of coding data. The techniques we introduce in this step are only suggestions. They capture the essential work of coding and have been used successfully. But there are many, many ways to code data. You will develop your own coding technique. For example, Valerie developed a technique with her students to analyze survey data that did not require Google Forms or Survey Monkey.

When Valerie's students collected survey data from Hispanic immigrants about their use of transportation to get to work and access health care and a supermarket, their survey included 21 questions and was answered by 89 respondents. Some of the questions had up to five possible responses, which meant that each question with multiple answers needed to be represented on a Google spreadsheet (which is also automatically generated by Google). To handle this volume of data, the students divided the survey into four sections and worked in teams logging the responses. After they had started, they realized they needed to develop a consistent shorthand to use to enter the data because when a data set was represented in a graph or pie chart, any differences in the way that an answer was recorded into the spreadsheet created a new column or section in the pie. For example, a recorded response Male and a recorded response M resulted in two answers rather than one, and that proved confusing. It took some time, but students went back and cleaned the data to standardize the shorthand and consolidate the data so that it was accurate, consistent, and readable.

When the raw data was shared with the Executive Director of the Community Resource Center, she asked that the data be even more compressed. For example, it was cumbersome to analyze data that reported that respondents traveled on bicycles, walked, took a bus, a train, drove a car, or took a carpool to work. So, the categories for transportation types were simplified to address these issues. Walking and bicycling were described as self-transport, any type of driving was described as a motor vehicle, and trains and buses were renamed as public transport. Once the data was simplified, it was much easier to see the frequencies that the charts described. The students then cut up hard copies of the charts (which were labeled with the question that they answered) and on a table top they moved the charts around to see what might emerge by putting different pieces of data in proximity to one another. Although this method could be done electronically, the students liked the flexibility of moving the chart copies around to see relationships that they might not have otherwise considered.

ASSESSMENT

Formative Assessment

Peer Assessment: Peer Panel. If you have divided your class into groups to identify key findings (or if more than one class is working on the same *TfC* project), a peer panel is an excellent way to decide which findings will go in your report. A peer panel allows students to experience the process by which the community of researchers decides what research will be published. Panels can be made up of classmates, older students, community members, or even faculty at nearby colleges. Student groups can be asked to present their three key findings and convince the panel that their key findings should be included in a final report/presentation.

Teacher Assessment: Checklist (survey data). Background for this assessment might include both introducing the Five-Step Techniques for coding survey data and illustrating how to use these skills with survey data from previous years or from the Internet. Then, have students in groups or individually use the instructions in the Five-Steps as a sequence to analyze and identify key findings for *their* survey data.

The work of data analysis may be broadly applied to STEM topics, social studies, or English classes. If your students are generating data through classroom, community, or lab research, it may take several class periods to complete. In those cases, we suggest using one of the following formative learning assessments at the end of the process:

Journal entries. Some sample prompts:
- Come up with your own list of steps for finding patterns in data.
- Write a note to a friend explaining how to identify surprising responses in data.

Checkpoints. Sample prompts:
- What was your or your group's most surprising finding?
- What was the hardest part about looking for patterns?
- Why do researchers code data?

OR

Checklist (focus group/interview data/fact pattern/or experiment results). Background for this assignment might include introducing the Four-Step Technique for coding textual responses and experimental results—such as interview and focus group transcripts. Then have students in groups or individually use the Four-Step Analysis Technique as a guide to analyze and identify key findings for their focus group, interview responses, or curricular experiments. The work of analysis may take several class periods. We would suggest using one of the following formative assessments at the end of each class.

Journal entries. Some sample prompts:
- Come up with your own list of steps for finding patterns in data.
- Write a note to a friend explaining how to identify surprising responses in data.

Checkpoints. Some sample prompts:
- What was your or your group's most surprising finding?
- Someone offers you a million dollars to answer this question: "What was the hardest part about looking for patterns?" What do you say?
- So, why do researchers code data?

Summative Assessment

Performance Tasks: Individual/Group Performance. After examining how another *TfC* class wrote their *Analysis and Findings* section for their final report/presentation (which may be found on the resource page of the *TfC* website), have students write a first draft of a newspaper article that highlights their findings and explains why the public should care about these findings. Then, edit and revise this draft for submission to a local newspaper for publication. This newspaper article may also be used as the basis for the *Analysis and Findings* section of the class's final report or presentation.

> *Individual/group performance. Here are two performance tasks to extend and apply the analytical skills learned in this step:*
> * Describe your experiences using the *TfC* techniques for coding. Then revise the technique for analyzing the results of your data analysis so that the technique works better for students in the future.
> * Identify a problem in your life, the life of your family, or in your circle of friends. Conduct informal interviews (with informed consent) and collect and record responses to your questions in bullet format. Analyze the data and identify key findings.

We advise focusing on the process of identifying a challenge that students care about and analyzing it, *not* on how students present their findings. Hence, it may be useful for students to know that this work will not be shared, and they will not be asked to put additional time into making a formal presentation. (So often, presentations become ends in themselves, in part because they are less demanding than analysis, or challenging our students to play the research.) We suggest reminding students of the structure of data collection and analysis and have them complete this assignment in their notebooks.

Making Curricular Connections

People in many fields and professions need to distinguish between what is critical and what is merely interesting. They then must convey this to their audience.

Write a two-page essay, a 2-minute talk, a 30-minute free write, or make a journal entry comparing the work of analyzing data in this *TfC* step to *one* of the following:

1. The concluding paragraph of a persuasive essay.
2. The concluding or summary section of a chapter in your history textbook.
3. The final section/paragraph of a great speech.
4. The concluding chapter of a work of nonfiction.
5. The conclusion section of your most recent report in your biology/chemistry lab notebook.

6. The final paragraph of a recent DBQ you have completed in a social studies class.

Here are some questions to structure this assignment:

- How do the authors/speakers decide what their key point or finding is?
- What are the major differences and similarities in how authors/speakers communicate their key point or finding to their audience?
- What is the role of the reader/listener in these examples above?
  - » Passive—being told: "Here are the key points; write them down!"
  - » Interactive—being encouraged to think along with the author/ speaker as they tease out or develop the key points.
  - » Somewhere in between passive and interactive.

FREQUENTLY ASKED QUESTIONS

Q. In recent times, there has been a growing distrust of experts. Moreover, data and evidence do not seem to have the same ability to persuade as they once did. How do we continue to support the importance of responsible data analysis in a world of alternative facts and unsubstantiated information?

A. We agree that data doesn't always persuade today, especially in regard to public issues. But we see this as a relative, not an absolute, decline. It is still easier to persuade someone who doesn't agree with you with an evidence-based argument than with an opinion or a threat. Moreover, governments, finance, industry, and nonprofits continue to make decisions and assess the effectiveness of these decisions based on evidence. Indeed, this is truer than it has ever been. Having said that, it is important for students to understand the limits of data. Today, we are struck by the fact that many people simply *can't see themselves in the data* that is used in political decision-making. This is true in regard to everything from the economic benefits of globalism to the health benefits of vaccinations. This reflects a failure within the research community, a community in which your students are joining.

Addressing the tendency to *not* see people in our data is part of the ethical duty of researchers, including your students. There are opportunities throughout the *TfC* research process to broaden the range of people who can see their life conditions and issues in both research and findings that result from responsible studies. The importance of surfacing and using individual perspectives, Step 1, lies in the fact those perspectives help ensure that the full range of voices and realities in your classroom and community shape the research process from the beginning. Similarly, in designing your data collection, Step 4, the goal, especially when doing survey research, is to have a sample or group of research participants that, together, reflect your school or community. Then, the task is to do everything to make it easy for these participants to be honest.

In this step, we urge you to identify and publicize a range of findings: some of which represent the views of the majority respondents; others that reveal a surprising, but strongly held perspective that exists among a smaller group of respondents. Finally, in advancing and enacting interpretations, recommendations, and/or policies based on your analysis, Step 7, we recommend that you consider the range of ethical perspectives in your community, and the different ways people understand what is right, just, and good when developing and seeking to publicize research-based insights or implement policy recommendations.

eTOOLBOX: RESOURCES

A range of resources for this step—including, hints, activities, lecture outlines, and samples of student work—may be found on the resource page of the *TfC* website: https://www.tools4changeseminar.com/resources.html

Implementation
Putting New Knowledge to Use

The *TfC* method culminates when students bring new knowledge to bear on their curriculum, communities, and lives. By "knowledge," we mean both the skills and dispositions and the information students develop by doing empirical research. Whether this knowledge has been developed in a semester or yearlong community research project or in shorter experiments or research exercises, it is meant to be used.

The challenge that runs throughout this guide, the challenge of playing the research game, is especially daunting when teachers try to help their students use the knowledge they have acquired. How can you help your students apply and refine the skills and dispositions they are learning? How do you bring the information your students have discovered through the research process—such as the realization that the food pantries in town are competing against one another in regard to food collection and financial support—to bear on the challenges outside the classroom? And, how do you bring knowledge to bear, given the constraints imposed by the class syllabus, the school day, the academic calendar, and your own life, especially when you have already stretched mightily to introduce your students to research?

In this *TfC* step, we discuss how—within the existing grammar of schooling—you can help your students put skills, dispositions, and information to use.

CASE STUDIES

The two case studies that follow illustrate how high school students that Bill and Valerie have worked with have brought research knowledge to bear on community challenges. The through line in both cases is that decisions about how and when to use research findings are based on a cluster of factors: time, context, stakeholders' needs, logistics, and established processes that are already in place.

In the first case study, we revisit a semester-long research project focused on hunger in the community that was first introduced in Step 2. There, we described how student conversations with town officials led them to focus on the challenge of hunger, in part because the town was already working on this issue. After extensive discussions aimed at refining their research question, the students framed the following question: How do community organizations address hunger in the Town of Rye and Westchester County in today's challenging environment?

After conducting their focus groups, students analyzed their data and then recorded the process of analysis for the report they wanted to present to town officials. The decision to write a draft of their proposed *Analysis and Findings* section of the report before deciding how the findings would be used was intentional. Bill knew that the process of organizing and writing this section would require that the students understand what the data was telling them. And, if they did this work of organizing and writing with the knowledge in the back of their minds that the next step was to decide how to act on their findings, their policy recommendations would be more thoughtful.

As work progressed, Bill and his students identified three key findings in the data:

1. *Awareness*, need for greater awareness about hunger in the community.
2. *Logistics,* the challenge of efficiently managing and distributing food resources and preventing waste among and between organizations focused on hunger.
3. *Coordination*, the need for greater coordination and consultation between community organizations.

Bill then divided the class into teams and asked each team to complete the following task: "Pick one or two of the three key findings and develop a list of action items." Here is what one team produced:

Resource

Policy Recommendations Team #2

- Recommendations for coordination and waste (we believe that if communication improved, then the issue of waste could be addressed):
    1. The government of the Town of Rye might encourage communication between these organizations and also be a liaison between groups when needed.
    2. Develop a scheduling system for each food pick-up day.
        a. Some backup notice system—via text or voicemail—so that if food is not picked up at a restaurant or store by the designated organization, another organization can get the food.
        b. Final backup system is that the restaurant or store gives food out at the back, and only those with an ID from the designated food pantry can get food.
            i. A database keeps count of how many times an organization picks up so that many organizations can participate.

ii. This method requires that organizations give out IDs and that restaurants and stores are informed of how the process works. This might make this recommendation a bit hard to implement as it requires a lot of work from the private sector, whose main concern is making money, not helping others.

3. Weekly/monthly meetings of the organizations battling hunger, with the Town of Rye officials present, so everyone can share perspectives. Having a few nutritionists attend would also be ideal to make sure that the health perspective is represented. Here are some possible goals for these meetings:

  a. Share personal contact information.
  b. Share concerns and issues so organizations solve problems as partners.
  c. Build familiarity so one organization could ask for assistance and support from the other organizations.
  d. Reaffirm unity—for example, this is not an individual competition for funding, but rather a team effort to defeat hunger.

The class then discussed the action items that team #2 produced. Then members of the class were asked to select an action item that came closest to meeting the following criteria:

- Would it work or be successful among the organizations working on hunger in the town?
- Is the work of implementing this recommendation doable for us as a class—that is, what honestly is our capacity?
- What impact would it have in the community?

Deciding on the action items to focus on required wisdom that emerged through give and take between Bill and the students. This give and take sounded like this: "That will take longer than you think." "Would the groups really go for that?" "Why would you think they would work together, when some of them have been successful competing for resources." The final version of the Policy Recommendation section of their report (next Resource) illustrates the conclusions from this conversation.

Resource

Policy Recommendations: We offer these recommendations with the humility that is appropriate for researchers who are just beginning to understand a complex issue such as hunger. Depending on the availability of resources, we want to continue our work on hunger next fall and spring through the Tools for

Change program. Additionally, we hope to help implement some of these policy recommendations by having some members of the Tools for Change research team participate in the Town of Rye's summer internship program. At least one member of the present Tools for Change class will be applying for the program this summer.

Our initial policy recommendation challenges members of our research team to act. One of our respondents reminded us of the importance of developing a personal understanding of the issue of hunger in the community. There are many reasons why a personal understanding is critical. First, hunger cannot be understood without respectfully and empathetically engaging with those who are living with hunger day in and day out. Grasping hunger in this way makes it easier to begin to understand the nature and complexity of the problem. Comprehending the nuances of the issues involved in fighting hunger also improves our sensitivity as researchers. The empathy and understanding that personal contact brings to a researcher makes the work of addressing community challenges more effective. Addressing community challenges such as hunger requires thinking, doing, and deep understanding. These mindsets and behaviors cannot be developed without authentic engagement. While some members of the Tools for Change research team are already involved with community kitchens in the area, the rest of our team—both teachers and students—pledge themselves to understand hunger in a personal way through volunteering at pantries and kitchens. Ethically, we can't expect other people to act virtuously if we don't.

Our second policy recommendation builds on one of the observations made several times by members of our focus groups: All organizations involved in this work need to be talking to each other on a regular basis. We strongly suggest that a monthly lunch meeting be established that brings together leaders of community kitchens, food pantries, and other local organizations that are addressing food insecurity in our community. Initially, these luncheons might foster and deepen relationships between leaders in the field. Over time, it might be possible for these leaders to begin to discuss common challenges and develop coordinated responses to these challenges. Students in our research team are willing to help with the logistics of setting up luncheon meetings if Town of Rye officials and/or business and civic leaders agree to sponsor these events and if local leaders who work in the hunger sector are willing to participate. The strongest ethical argument for hosting these lunch meetings is that it will improve the situation for all people working in the area of hunger in the community. One of our challenges will be to convince people that working to improve the overall, long-term situation is worth taking time away from their own good work and that this overall improvement can actually happen.

The Town of Rye agreed to cohost a meeting, but wisely thought that the first meeting should not be planned around lunch. Here is a copy of the letter that the students drafted inviting organizations to the first meeting cohosted with the Town of Rye.

Resource

Dear _____,

On behalf of the Town of Rye and the Tools for Change seminar, we invite you to attend a meeting of the leaders of all the food pantries and soup kitchens that serve the Town of Rye.

This spring both the students in the Tools for Change seminar and officials in the Town of Rye studied the extent of hunger in the Town. Visits were made to all the food pantries and soup kitchens. One of the findings from the preliminary research report prepared by the Tools for Change students suggests that there may be important benefits in having the leaders involved in this work meet to get to know one another better, share information, and consider additional ways to collaborate. The Town's own report reached the same conclusion. (Copies of both reports are attached.)

We appreciated the information you provided. We would like to share all of our findings with you and receive your feedback at this meeting.

Please let us know if you, or someone from your organization, is available to attend a meeting on either: Wednesday, September 17 at 5:00 P.M. OR Thursday, September 18 at 10:00 A.M. In either case, the meeting will be held on the 3rd floor, Town of Rye, Town Hall, 10 Pearl Street in Port Chester.

Some months later, one of Valerie's classes read the report that Bill's class produced and decided to act on the first recommendation—that is, to make an effort to understand hunger in a personal manner. They framed the following question: How do the actions of volunteers influence food donor participation at food collection points? Early on in this work, students suggested that the best way to gather the evidence to answer their questions about volunteer experiences was to go out and work alongside other volunteers. The class formed teams and contacted hunger service organizations to ask where leaders saw the greatest needs and where they felt the students would be most helpful. One organization asked the students to go to a supermarket to both participate in and evaluate a program the organization had created to encourage shoppers to directly contribute to addressing hunger in the community. The program had the following features: Volunteers at the front of the store asked patrons to pick up an "end hunger" shopping list at the entrance of a supermarket, select and purchase several items from the list, and then drop the items off with the volunteers as they exited the store. After several hours, the research team observed four things:

1. Despite the best efforts of the volunteers, shoppers did not understand what they were being asked to do.
2. Signage identifying the organization and purpose was too small to read.
3. No one staffed the drop-off table.
4. Volunteers did not look uniformly professional.

Valerie's students recorded the average amount of time between when customers were in earshot of the volunteers and when they entered the supermarket door. Additionally, they tracked the amount of food collected in 1 hour. They determined that volunteers had only 3 seconds to grab the attention of shoppers and hand them a list. To address this issue, the students wrote a script that efficiently standardized the process and appealed to the core message of the organization. "Please shop to feed hungry people." The students also noted the number of shopping lists that resulted in donations during the same time. The students told the food distribution leaders that they wanted to try putting two volunteers at the exit table to say "thank you" to patrons who dropped off grocery bags. Finally, the students remade the signage, placed it in a location where potential donors could easily see it, and made name tags for the volunteers with the food collection organization identified. (They also requested that volunteers wear a white shirt and jeans.) Implementing these recommendations helped to double the number of donations over the next several weeks.

KEY FEATURES

Researchers have both an ethical obligation and a strong desire to put the knowledge they have developed to use. The universities and colleges that many of your students will attend are committed to bringing knowledge to bear on the most important problems of our time. In fact, the federal government has granted them a tax exempt, nonprofit status, based on the expectation that they will serve the public. All universities and most colleges have stated explicitly that this public service includes—indeed, some have said, "begins"—with commitment to bring knowledge developed within the university to bear on challenges in society. Similarly, the professional communities that many of our students will join in the future have been granted great autonomy from government oversight in part because of the expectation that they will share expertise and information for the good of society.

Our students are also committed to improving the world they live in. Today, this commitment is increasingly evident by the actions of students in every conceivable field, from sustainability to school and community safety. The deep desire within so many of our students to have a positive impact can find an analytical and ethical expression in this step of the *TfC* method. As a society, we have not provided outlets for students to make analytical and ethical contributions to their schools and communities. Indeed, high school students have traditionally satisfied the desire to make a contribution to society by physical actions as members of clubs in school and performing service and volunteering outside of school—collecting gently worn clothes for those in need and giving of their time at soup kitchens or as mentors. Anyone who has seen the smile on the face of a 6-year-old who is lacing up ice skates for the very first time with his high school mentor knows that this kind of service and volunteering has great impact.

TfC is animated by the belief that high school students can *also* have an impact by taking the new information their thinking and doing has uncovered and sharing it with individuals and organizations that might benefit from it and/or collaboratively addressing a challenge in their community, and/or using research skills to investigate new problems.

PLANNING

This step is designed to help teachers use knowledge developed through research in two contexts:

1. *In the classroom* to identify ways to easily and strategically use the information their students have developed in short empirical exercises to update and enliven the curriculum.
2. *In the community* as the policy implementation phase in semester or yearlong *TfC* community research or relevant PBL, service, or experiential education projects in which students develop recommendations from their findings and collaboratively implement these recommendations.

Whether in the classroom or in the community, the challenge is to put knowledge to work. Next, we describe the planning involved in both classroom-based and community-focused efforts to use knowledge developed during the research process.

Using Research Knowledge: Short Research Experiments and Curricular Exercises

The *TfC* research method reaches its culmination when students use the knowledge—either in terms of skills and dispositions or information—they have acquired. Both the experience of doing research and the knowledge—however modest—that this research has produced can be used in your classroom. First, knowledge can be used by communicating the information contained in the answers to your question to those beyond your classroom and school who might have an interest or can benefit from it. Second, knowledge may be used by creating opportunities to refine and develop the research thinking, and doing that, students have been introduced to in brief curriculum-based exercises.

Bringing Knowledge to Others. When data answers a research question, new knowledge is created. While it is more common to think of knowledge creation as a process that happens only in a lab, short curricular-inspired research can also produce knowledge. In the classroom, this process sounds like this: "When we interviewed our grandparents who are currently receiving Social Security payments, we found that less than 10 percent knew that Social Security was part of the New Deal"; or this: "Our hypothesis was that views on animal cloning would be related to age—that is, younger people would be more open to the idea. This is, in fact, what our short survey of classmates and parents revealed."

In short classroom empirical exercises, this new knowledge will not be definitive and you and your students should, of course, be honest about the limited nature of the experiments that produced it. But this knowledge can and should be used because that is the best way for students to see how new knowledge changes the world around them.

TfC classes use the knowledge they have developed to connect, inspire, and assist individuals and organizations that may or should have an interest in what you and your students have discovered. In curricular-inspired experiments, this will often take the form of using the new knowledge to converse with the curriculum. Curriculum across the disciplines is often perceived to be neutral, objective information or worse, simply vocabulary. Bringing new knowledge, especially knowledge students have discovered themselves, to bear on the curriculum is another way to create an interactive relationship between students and what they are learning.

When a U.S. history class in a wealthy suburb found that 60 percent of the parents surveyed believed that the New Deal was an example of socialism, it prompted students to talk back to the textbook:

- Why did the author of the textbook say that the New Deal was a reform— what did they base this characterization on?
- Did socialism mean the same in 1933 as it does today?
- What definition of socialism were the authors of the textbook using? What definition should historians of the New Deal use?

For some students, bringing new knowledge to bear on their curriculum can help to demystify textbook information. For example, it becomes clear to many *TfC* students that information finds its way into their textbook through a process similar to the one they have undertaken.

Some curriculum-based research can yield knowledge that can be brought to bear on issues beyond the curriculum and outside the classroom. The teachers we have worked with are always looking to find ways for their students to forge connections beyond the school that are doable as well as educational. Here are some examples of how your students can use the new knowledge they have developed to make connections beyond the classroom.

- *Short interviews* with senior citizens about their memories of the Korean War might be used as the basis for a student presentation in your classroom, in a retirement community, or in a letter to an historian of the Korean War to see if the student's findings are consistent with that of the historian.
- *An analysis of the comments* left by readers of a newspaper article on genetically modified crops might prompt a letter to the curator of the comments section, informing her of what their analysis reveals about the readers of the newspaper.

- *A class that surveyed members of the community about policing might meet with the police chief* to share their findings and/or inquire if these findings were consistent with the police department's own community outreach.
- *The case study in Step 6 that used a log of family expenses* to give students practice analyzing qualitative data could be used to compare the information students generated with data on monthly expenses of families in their city.

These examples illustrate that putting knowledge to use need not require elaborate planning or take up large amounts of time. Indeed, in most cases, what is required—and we recognize this is no small ask—is a small team of teachers who want to undertake this work and head these implementation efforts. Moreover, these examples allow students to build a range of so-called "soft skills" such as the ability to communicate with adults, speak in public, and design presentations that work outside of school. They also offer opportunities for students to practice image management—all in the service of bringing knowledge to bear in an authentic and genuine manner.

Using Research Skills and Dispositions. "I didn't know I liked research until I interviewed my grandfather." "Now that I know how to do a survey, I have a question I want to survey people about." We hear comments like this from our students all the time. What we, and the teachers we have worked with, have come to know is that even a brief research experience—interviewing a relative, observing how people of different ages physically interact in a public place—can have an impact on a student. It can help them realize that they have an interest or a gift they had not been aware of before. A short research experience can also introduce students to methods and techniques that they can refine and use to address their own questions and concerns. This is what happened to Nanfu Wang. Wang's award-winning documentary on China's one child policy, *One Child Nation*, began with a simple, informal interview with her mother.

Many teachers and schools are expanding research opportunities for all students. Once the initial stretch is made to introduce research, it is easier to consider creating additional opportunities to practice and refine research skills. Teachers have frequently started this work after seeing the effect that brief research experiences have had on their students. This helps them recognize more clearly that the best way for middle and high school students to develop college-level skills is by starting to do what college students do (or are supposed to do). Some schools have encouraged all teachers to use short empirical research exercises to deepen engagement with the curriculum. Others have integrated research experiences into the life of the school in creative ways—for example, developing a school improvement team from among the members of the student council and asking them to undertake empirical research to address a school challenge.

Rye Neck School District Integrating Research Across the Middle and High School Years. When Bill and Valerie first met in Bill's Tools for Change interdistrict community program in the Town of Rye, New York, a Schoolwide Enrichment Model (SEM) was already in place in her school. SEM is a research-based "blueprint" for school district enhancement that is used as a framework for the types of learning experiences students have in and out of school. There are similar programs in districts across the country. In Valerie's district, SEM is used with a wide variety of talent development programs that reflect the sciences, humanities, and the arts. When Valerie brought a group of high school students to a *TfC* class, she was struck by the level of engagement they exhibited and the community support the program received. She started thinking of how *TfC* might work with SEM.

Over the next several years with the active support of her then principal, now superintendent, Dr. Barbara Ferraro, the Board of Education, administrators, teachers, and community members, Valerie built a district-wide K–12 integrated social science research program in her district. Here, we focus on the recursive research opportunities that Rye Neck provides for its middle and high school students. In the Rye Neck Middle School, all students in grades 7 and 8 take a semester-long PBL course that meets on alternate days. Students select a "researchable" personal interest (it may be a global issue but must show up locally) and they then develop and present a research project based on a research question and a five-step process:

1. History—What happened in the past that informs the current status of the topic?
2. Current status—What is going now?
3. Field Experts—Who is doing research or working in the field that the topic describes?
4. Publications and Organizations—What kinds of questions and conversations are experts involved in? Where do people in the field go for information? How is that information presented?
5. Future trends in the field of study.

Additionally, students must engage in a literature review, conduct two interviews with field experts, and are encouraged to collect data typically via a survey. PBL students also build models, create demonstrations, and use videos to help them communicate what they find. The school librarian is a frequent presence in PBL and content classes in the middle and high school to familiarize students with Noodle Tools (research tracking software). The benefit of introducing information management helps students to capture their ideas while they conduct a literature review and learn to converse with other researchers through academic articles.

At the high school level, Rye Neck's opportunities expand to include an elective credit in a *TfC* course called Action Research for Community Change. Action Research students work as a research consulting team on *TfC* projects that have

benefited many community organizations. In addition, an existing science research program has been linked to both AP Capstone and the *TfC* program. This
has greatly expanded student interest in concurrently exploring science and social
science around related topics. For example, one student used the science research
program to study gut bacteria while simultaneously participating on a *TfC* research project that investigates patients' perceptions of their relationships with
doctors—a topic she cared about and one that reflected her longer-term career
goal of becoming a doctor. Finally, Rye Neck students often present their research
to local organizations and governmental panels.

Finally, at Rye Neck, *TfC* is also used as the core of the Independent Learner
Program (ILP), an elective course in which students conduct individual research
projects. On average, there are more than 40 research projects running concurrently. Some of these projects are shorter term and school-based and others take
place in the community and operate for an academic year or more.

Bringing New Knowledge to the Community: Semester and Yearlong Research Projects

Today, many of our students desperately want to make a positive street-level impact in their neighborhoods. We have found that the strongest motivation for
teachers to fully engage with the work of bringing knowledge (students have acquired by answering their research question) to bear in their communities is the
desire to honor their students' desire to improve their communities. Developing
a plan of action—or policy recommendations—based on your findings and collaboratively working to implement at least one of these recommendations is the
most effective way to begin to tackle your community challenge and recognize
the often-enormous integrity your students bring to this work.

The Importance of Relationships and Collaboration. We have learned
through years of experience that students can only bring new knowledge to bear
on a community challenge if they are actively engaged in the community. This
is especially true when it comes to implementing a plan of action based on your
findings. The ability that you and your students have to move from the key findings you discovered in your data to change on the ground usually depends on
your capacity to deepen a relationship you made earlier in the research process
and/or develop new respectful strategic partnerships with individuals, organizations, and/or government officials.[1]

Building and/or deepening relationships in the community becomes easier
over time and can be done sequentially. Indeed, it is important for you, as a teacher with multiple classes and (possibly) hundreds of students, to know that in
most cases you only need a single community partner (especially if it is an organization) to help your students put their new knowledge to use. It is certainly true
that many adults and community organizations don't take high school students
seriously enough for a working relationship to develop. We have found, however,

that when students are respectful, honest about what they don't know, and can bring evidence-based recommendations to the table, community organizations are more willing to have an initial conversation. Over the years, the teachers we have worked with have been surprised at how eager government (at all levels) and nonprofit organizations—such as the NAACP, YMCA, the local League of Women Voters—are to collaborate with our students if approached respectfully and with assistance that clearly helps them. Undoubtedly, there are opportunities like this in your community, some of which you may have explored earlier in your research. Make a call and/or have your students reach out to organizations that you think would be good collaborators.

Community Problem Solving Takes Time: Look for Small Victories Along the Way. Even after you have willing community partners, the work of developing and implementing a plan of action invariably moves more slowly than you or your students may wish. For the sake of our students, we desperately wish that change came quickly. But a large part of honoring the integrity of our students is to be honest about the efforts of those who have worked on these problems before them—in some cases before they were born. Honesty also extends to illustrating what community change looks like, feels like, and how long it can take.

This honesty starts with recognizing or, more accurately, reiterating that addressing community safety or hunger is an adaptive challenge. That is, safety and hunger are problems that do not have a right answer that can be easily discovered and quickly applied. They are, instead, open-ended problems, in which solutions must be forged over time and with others. Put differently, very few community challenges are technical in nature—that is, very few community problems can be solved simply by creating a mobile app and presenting it to the mayor and declaring victory.

By their very nature, most *TfC* community challenges must be tackled thoughtfully, collaboratively, and over time. A wiser, and yes, more effective approach, then, is to help students become aware that (community) change takes time by pointing out how long it took for scientific discoveries to be made, for history to unfold. In the case of semester or yearlong community-based research, it is advisable to devise and implement policy recommendations that allow you and your students to *contribute* to addressing—as distinct from "solving"—the problem at hand within the time available.

What does a contribution look like and will this contribution satisfy your students' need to make an impact? The answer to these questions is, yes. The key is to build into your policy or action plan opportunities for small authentic accomplishments along the way. These accomplishments can range from a meeting with a city official to discuss how to work together to a letter to the editor that highlights impediments. In the Citizenship Lab at Duke University, undergraduates and refugee high school students worked for an academic year to improve bus stop seating in the city.[2] Students first conducted interviews with bus riders. The key findings from these interviews was that—more than anything—riders wanted a place to sit while waiting for the bus. When transit officials continued to focus on the reasons why they could not act quickly, and impediments to addressing the issue, the team developed a three-step action plan. Each of the three steps involved an action that moved the work forward and could be celebrated as an accomplishment in its own right. Here are the three steps that students were proud to view as small victories:

1. Students built inexpensive "bus cubes" to both provide a place for weary riders to sit and to spark a community conversation about the state of bus stops in the city. Students then had the satisfaction of placing these cubes around the city.
2. Students wrote an op-ed calling for a different approach to bus stop improvement.
3. Students prepared and presented a research memo designed to remind city and transit officials that they needed, above all, to respond to the urgency their riders felt about the issue of bus stop seating.

Over the course of many months, these steps did eventually result in the introduction of new bus seating in the city, but student moral remained high because the project featured intermediate outcomes.

As the experience of the students in Citizenship Lab suggests, viewing the work of implementing recommendations as a multistage process also acknowledges that community change is not linear. Often, the implementation process continues after the class has ended. Indeed, we have found again and again that a small group of students will take it upon themselves to continue the work as part of a future social studies or civics class, in a teacher-led club, as part of a summer internship, or even on their own time.

Bill and Valerie have both worked with students who are so motivated by their involvement in *TfC* and so deeply invested in the importance of doing something with their findings that they have voluntarily continued to work within their communities, even after the seminar has officially ended. Whether it is a group of students who develop a one-page flyer with evidence-based advice for high school jobseekers or a student led effort to use survey findings to encourage their school counselors and teachers to focus more on what college work actually *looks like* (instead of how to get into college) many *TfC* students don't see the work as ending when the class ends. Imagine a project in which students can't stop working even after the school year has ended!

Two Planning Tasks

To help you adopt this wise and effective approach to your classroom, we discuss the two critical tasks involved in this step:

1. Moving from key findings to policy recommendations.
2. Collaboratively implementing policy recommendations.

From Findings to Policy Recommendations. Three questions will orient the work of translating key findings into policy recommendations:

1. Which one or two of your key findings can be the basis for action to address the community challenge that inspired your research project?
2. Who or what organizations can help you act? And/or what organizations serve people who are dealing with the underlying challenge you are focusing on?
3. How can your awareness of the ethical dimension of this challenge increase your chances of being successful in the implementation step?
   - What is the strongest ethical argument for the action or recommendation you propose?
   - What is the strongest ethical argument against the action or recommendation you propose?
   - How will you incorporate the answers to these questions in your strategy?

Collaboratively Implementing Policy Recommendations. There are many ways that you can move from recommendations to action. Below are examples of policy actions and recommendations that illustrate the range of approaches *TfC* classes have taken to implement their policy recommendations.

1. *Policy action/recommendation*: Share key findings that would help individuals or organizations working in the field.

   ### Example of Implementation:
   - A team shared findings from six in-depth interviews with individual social workers working with homeless families with the entire county social work team.
   - A team shared findings on changing demographics among seniors with a range of private organizations focused on enhancing the quality of life for seniors in the community.

Resource

Below, find a flyer that a small group of *TfC* students produced to help high school students in their community find jobs. As the flyer indicates, the "hints" for young jobseekers were based on more than 200 *TfC* surveys completed by students in the area and interviews with employers.

LOOKING FOR A JOB?[3] Are the odds in your favor?
Students in Tools for Change, a high school research team, spoke with other high school students and employers in the area and found[4] that many high school students looking for jobs hear the answer NO when

they seek employment! Here are 5 Simple Things You Can Do to Improve Your Odds:

- *Presentation.* Focus on how you present yourself. The employers we spoke with said it wasn't a lack of experience or grades that made them decide not to hire a teen. Instead, it was that the applicant did not seem mature or did not dress professionally.
- *Personality.* Most of the employers, especially those in sales-related businesses, stressed the importance of having a friendly personality. This means someone who can interact with both fellow employees and customers.
- *Flexibility.* Many of the employers we spoke with said that one of the main reasons why they didn't hire someone our age was because the applicant had very little time available to work. Don't expect an employer to accommodate your schedule, especially if you are including hobbies and "down time" as times you absolutely can't work.
- *Knowledge.* Before applying for a job, it is important to do some research and gain an understanding of the company, their goals, and image. This information will help you to understand the kinds of employees the company is looking for and you will have a better interview if you can demonstrate your interest in what they do by showing you have done some homework. Making this effort will also allow you to find a job that is right for you.
- *Network.* Let your friends and adults know you are looking for work. Ask people your family knows, coaches, teachers, and religious leaders to let you know if they hear about jobs. Employers often fill jobs with people they know and trust. If you are not surrounded by adults (and even if you are), be aggressive in looking for jobs. Walk into stores (by yourself) and ask for an application or an interview. If you haven't heard back from an employer in a while, call them and find out if they have looked at your application. Employers want to hire people who want to work.

2. *Policy action/recommendation.* Partner with a community organization or with local government units to collaboratively implement a recommendation:

   ### Examples of implementation:
   - A study on public perceptions of the quality of local drinking water was used by the Town of Mamaroneck, New York, to combat negative advertising designed to shake public confidence in the water supply.
   - An individual student surveyed members of her church to assess the needs of their faith community in advance of selecting a new pastor.

3. *Policy action/recommendation.* Use findings to spread or deepen awareness about a critical community issue.

Example of implementation:

- Members of a team in Newark, New Jersey, met with city officials and appeared on a community television show to discuss what their focus groups revealed about how community and family impact high school students.
- A team shared, with a community organization that advocates for the rights of undocumented workers, findings on challenges that migrant families faced in traveling to work, accessing health care, and shopping for food.

4. *Policy action/recommendation*: Partner with community organizations or with local government so that *TfC* students can execute an action plan.

Examples of implementation:

- A team worked with the local government officials to create a paid internship program to enable *TfC* students and other high school students in the community to help implement a report that found service-oriented community organizations would be more effective if they used social media more intelligently.

Resource

This is an example of how a TfC team partnered with government officials in the Town of Rye, New York, to launch a paid summer internship program. The program was designed in part as a means to implement recommendations regarding social media and civic engagement that a *TfC* seminar had developed. As the announcement below indicates, two of the initial interns were matched with local community organizations to help them use social media to increase their effectiveness. The internship program is still in operation and continues to offer a structure for students to implement *TfC* policy recommendations and address other challenges in the community.

Town of Rye: Tools for Change Summer Internship Program

Project #1: Social Media Workshop for Model American Community Organizations—Two Interns
Student interns would develop a social media-civic engagement workshop that would be offered to organizations in conjunction with the Town of Rye Model American Communities seminar series. If—after the workshop—any of the organizations wanted the advisory group to implement a social media

project, the group would schedule additional meetings with the organization through the intern supervisor.

Project #2: Social Media for the Town of Rye—Two Interns

- Student interns would provide social media strategies for the Town of Rye.
- Update and revise the town's Facebook page and website in a manner consistent with the requirements of a governmental social media website.
- Research other forms of social media and suggest possible implementation strategies.

Project #3: Research—African American Cemetery—Two Interns

- Students would provide research for the African American cemetery.
- The students would research and document the cultural significance of the cemetery to the community and establish a preservation plan for the cemetery while highlighting its educational value for students, citizens, and visitors.

Program: Six Interns

- 6-week program: July 9–August 17
- 6 hours/week; days and times to be determined with interns
- $5 hourly stipend

Apply by June 29 to Dave Thomas.

5. *Policy action/recommendation*: Use the *TfC* method to address another issue of concern.

Examples of implementation (all under the direction of Valerie):

- A study examined how perceptions of adolescent, educated girls in Syria, Jordan, and Kuwait are connected to cultural norms and school life. (An Arabic-speaking student interviewed girls via Skype and phone.)
- A study examined the perceptions of 17- and 18-year-old female high school students to investigate their attitudes toward educational aspirations, marriage, and motherhood.

TEACHING

We, and the teachers we have been fortunate to work with, are grappling with how to find bandwidth to actually do the culminating step in the research process: bringing knowledge students have developed to bear in ways that are meaningful and consequential for them. Talking and telling does not help students understand how knowledge can shape the world they live in and empower them to start doing some shaping themselves. Instead, this requires venturing beyond the walls of the school and developing relationships in the community. This, of course, makes sense but—again—how best to do this in today's schools?

It is common to think of these ventures outside the school as special events that require mobilization and months of planning. Then when they are completed and celebrated, everything goes back to normal. We used to think that making it easier to pull off these special ventures was what was required. Working with teachers over the years has convinced us that the best way to make this easier is to encourage teachers and schools to shift the way they think about bringing knowledge to bear on the curriculum and community.

We want our students to make research a part of their way of being, something they do in the classroom but also in the course of their everyday lives. Is it possible that we, as teachers and administrators, can make inquiry a way of being in our classrooms and schools? That is to suggest that making research, in general, and the work of bringing knowledge to bear, in particular, routine.

We have tried to illustrate how using new knowledge can be accomplished in small and manageable ways or in large and more in-depth ways. Ultimately, it is not the size of the venture but how you approach it. Regarding community projects, we have found that the best approach is to begin with the end goal in mind. The end goal for Bill in the Citizenship Lab at Duke University and Valerie at Rye Neck High School is for community members and organizations to *seek out our students* so that they may tell them about the research needs they have, problems that require empirical research, or challenges they are encountering.

You can build a reputation for helpful research in your community so that people rely on you and your students and seek them out. This requires that you and your students approach opportunities to bring knowledge to bear with both an immediate and long-term perspective. The challenge is to view collaborative efforts to use new knowledge not as special one-time events, but as the beginning or the continuation of a long-term relationship within the community. With each project, large or small, your capacity and that of your students increases and so too does the web of relationships. This is how neighborhoods grow. Our schools can be sources of knowledge-based connection and collaboration in their neighborhoods.

ASSESSMENT

Formative Assessment

Free-Write and Share. After identifying actions/recommendations, have students spend 15 minutes responding to the following prompt:

> What actions outside of class should we take to implement one of our policy recommendations?

Then, have each student pair with a partner, read what they have written, and then ask their partner:

a. Would you participate in this action?
b. Why or why not?
c. If not, how could the action be changed so that you would participate?

Then, switch roles.

Teacher Assessment: Checklist. Have students choose one approach from the list of six ways that *TfC* classes have used to implement their findings. For example, *TfC* students have "used their findings to spread or deepen awareness of a critical community issue."

Then, have students create a checklist (preferably in rank order) of actions they should take to implement their findings using that approach. If, for example, they wish to use their findings to spread awareness about homelessness, how specifically will they do that, what actions will they need to take, and in what order?

Performance Tasks: Group Performance. After examining the list of the ways that *TfC* classes have worked with community partners to implement findings from their research, have student teams:

1. Examine their key findings and brainstorm a list of possible policy recommendations.
2. Choose the most promising policy recommendation and identify who (besides the students themselves) should act. Ideally, this would be an organization or person you have developed a relationship with earlier in the process. What should they do and why should they act now?
3. Then, choose the most appropriate action to move the work of implementation forward. Here are some steps that *TfC* teams have taken at this stage in their work:
   - Write a *letter* to an organization, making the case they should work with your class to implement one of your policy recommendations.
   - Write an *op-ed* piece for the local newspaper detailing what the challenge is, what should be done, who (in addition to the students) should act, and why they should act.
   - Organize a panel discussion to make the case for this implementation work. (Tasks here include publicity, logistics, inviting panelists, and meeting presentation—talking points, slide show, and so on.)

Summative Assessment

Final Evaluation. Here are the types of evidence that can be used to evaluate a student's learning:

- *Quality and effectiveness of final report/presentation and student's contribution.* The quality and effectiveness of the final report/presentation should impact each student's evaluation. It is hard to argue—no matter what the contribution—that an individual student can get an A, if the report and/ or presentation is of poor quality.
- *Success of collaborative policy implementation and student's contribution to this work.* It is hard to make the case that a student should get an A if nothing changes on the ground because of the project. Recall, however, there is a very wide range of outcomes that can have an impact on the ground.
- *Student self-assessment of their contribution to the group for semester or yearlong research project.* Revisit the *Self-Assessment Rubric* (Appendix A) and/or the *Seeing and Being Rubric* (Appendix B) that may have been used as a diagnostic or baseline at the beginning of the research process to enable students to assess their contributions over the course of the project. If applicable, have students take *Team Leadership Rubric* to assess research leadership (Appendix C).
- *Student interview or short paper* detailing how semester or yearlong research has affected their ethical principles, if they have been surfaced in Step 1— that is, challenged these principles, prompted them to refine or amend them, and so on.
- *Individual journal entries taken together.*
- *Portfolio*, which might include:
  - » *Performance Tasks* from informed consent letters to taped interviews to presentations.
  - » *Selected Assignments*—free writes, check points, and so on.
  - » *Draft, revisions, and final versions* of research tools: survey or interview questions and/or focus group prompts, or participant observation protocols.
  - » *Drafts, revisions, and final versions* of sections or complete reports and/ or presentations.

Making Curricular Connections

Choose one example of a social movement in U.S. history—Populism, Progressivism, and the Civil Rights Movement—and write a two-page memo (or a short talk) on one of the following topics:

a. What can we learn from this social movement that can help us collaboratively implement one of our policy recommendations?

    b. How do you define a successful social movement and then use that definition to assess our *TfC* implementation?

    c. Are some goals easier to realize in our democracy than others? If so, identify one easier short-term policy recommendation and one harder, long-term policy recommendation.

Making English Connections. Read the quote below and write a short persuasive essay or a 2-minute speech that answers the question: Who is right here, the teenager or the adult?

"Teenagers just want to wipeout racism and you (as an adult) are like, 'you are never going to do that, so let's just go out to eat.'"[5]

FREQUENTLY ASKED QUESTIONS

Q. How do you build relationships with community organizations?

A. Provide them with something they value and be reliable—that is, do what you say you will do. What providing value means will vary depending on the organization and group. For some organizations, simply offering the opportunity to meet and speak to young people is something of value. For many government units and NGOs, the optics of engaging with youth, alone, make it worthwhile for them to engage. Take advantage of their institutional needs. Over time, these interactions can deepen into opportunities to collect and share data. Other organizations might seek you and your students out to accomplish a specific goal that requires youth buy-in—for example, creating a summer internship program that would appeal to youth and allow them to work on projects they believe to be meaningful. Still, other organizations, especially those that are under-resourced, will respond positively to an offer to help them translate data into possible action items. Many organizations have done a good job of collecting data, but do not have the time or capacity to analyze it, let alone use the knowledge that emerges from this analysis to make recommendations that might improve the way their organizations operate. It is easy for an organization to say "yes" if the alternative is that the data will never be analyzed otherwise. Adding this kind of value does require that you, the teacher, fully participate in this work to ensure that it is of high quality.

eTOOLBOX: RESOURCES

A range of resources for this step—including, hints, activities, lecture outlines, and samples of student work—may be found on the resource page of the *TfC* website: https://www.tools4changeseminar.com/resources.html

Postscript

At the end of the day, after all our claims, examples, model activities, and evaluations—in short, all the evidence in support of this method have been listed—the primary reason teachers and students are drawn to *TfC* is because it *looks and feels right.* It looks and feels right at a time when so much that is related to the works and lives of our students doesn't look or feel right. We hope that the evidence makes it easier for principals, teachers, parents, and students to choose what is right.

It is as simple or as complicated as that.

Here, we arrive at exactly the place we hope our students end up: In possession of a well-tested method for understanding what new data can (and cannot do) for them, their schools, and their communities.

Self-Assessment Rubric[1]

Students: You may choose two (2) or three (3) elements from each rubric as criteria for class performance assessment purposes. Highlight bullets from each list.

Your choices will be considered as the basis for your grade, based on class assignments, class assessments, and any extra work that you do that helps advance our research.

Name _____

Marking Period _____

Date _____

Content Knowledge: Mastery of core concepts in social science research.

- I understand the context, history, and major issues of the method being studied.
- I understand and can apply the essential disciplinary concepts and skills.
- I understand the rules, definitions, and theories of the method being studied.
- I understand and can use disciplinary vocabulary accurately.
- I am able to answer questions in my own words and draw information from a range of sources relating to the topic or question being studied.
- ADD YOUR OWN . . .

Information, Communication, and Technology Skills: The skillful use of information, communication, and technology to enhance learning and demonstrate understanding.

- I listen critically and ask perceptive questions.
- I have the skills necessary to assess characteristics of an audience and tailor my communication accordingly, especially in regard to research reports and presentations.
- I have the skills necessary to speak and write with clarity, use appropriate vocabulary, and the conventions of the discipline in the social sciences.
- I am able to distinguish between well-researched, accurate, nonbiased information and information of questionable quality.

- I use visual media creatively to communicate meaning and enhance audiences' understanding.
- I use technology as a tool to research, organize, evaluate, and communicate the content.
- I know how to access information efficiently and effectively, evaluate information critically, and competently use information accurately and creatively.
- I possess a fundamental understanding of the ethical issues related to research from authorship to the protection of human subjects.
- I know how to cite sources within work products.
- ADD YOUR OWN . . .

Thinking and Doing: Cognitive and eta-cognitive skills, such as critical and creative thinking, problem solving, and positive "habits of mind." Habits of mind are those consistent strategies one applies to oneself when learning something new and as one strives to improve one's performance.

- I work effectively in an environment of ambiguity and uncertainty.
- I can demonstrate fluency, flexibility, originality, and can elaborate on experiences and knowledge to gain new perspectives.
- I reflect on and assess what we have learned or accomplished.
- I am able to predict the consequences of a research choice—for example, the choice of method.
- I can speculate and raise questions about what is not known.
- I can synthesize and integrate ideas, concepts, and inferences to form a cohesive argument or account.
- I can demonstrate understanding of the criteria used for an evaluation of data or an argument, and as appropriate, create my own criteria.
- I can apply understanding to new situations to add new insight.
- I demonstrate a disposition necessary for sustained intellectual curiosity.
- I am open to new experiences and perspectives.
- I understand my learning style and develop strategies to use them effectively to enhance my learning.
- ADD YOUR OWN . . .

Social and Emotional Skills: Self-regulation, interpersonal skills, personal and group productivity, and work habits.

- I can demonstrate my ability to work effectively with diverse teams.
- I am a leader who can leverage the collective intelligence of a team.
- I have a perspective that allows me to bridge cultural differences and use differing perspectives to increase the quality of our work.

- I exercise flexibility and a willingness to be helpful in making necessary compromises to accomplish a common goal.
- I assume shared responsibility for collaborative work in the lab.
- I am self-directed and manage resources effectively.
- I manage my time, prioritize tasks, set goals, and meet deadlines.
- I seek out feedback and am flexible and reasonable in receiving it.
- I use feedback to improve myself and revise work products.
- I demonstrate high standards of craftsmanship in work lab products and performances.
- I accept responsibility for my own work/behavior and I consider consequences and adjust my behavior accordingly.
- I treat others with respect and approach work with a positive attitude.
- I demonstrate integrity and ethical behavior.
- ADD YOUR OWN . . .

Seeing and Being Rubric

Image Management	Seminar Discussion	Assignments	Leadership	Above and Beyond
Student is prepared for class: Homework Materials Attitude.	Student has read required material and is prepared to volunteer reflective comments.	Assignments are complete and standard English spelling and grammar are used.	Student volunteers for the responsibility of organizing a research team.	Student reaches out to teacher to offer help with unassigned, necessary class work or management.
Student is respectful, responsive, appears alert, and maintains eye contact when others are speaking.	Student asks informed questions and connects the literature review to class prompts and comments from others.	Student collaborates with group members and is flexible in terms of including their ideas as well as those of others.	Student understands and communicates their role and ensures that others understand theirs.	Student voluntarily reaches out to assist classmates who may have challenges fully participating in the work of the lab. (Example: *ELL students)
Student's physical posture and behavior demonstrates an understanding of professional decorum.	Student applies prior knowledge and information from the literature review to reflect on and/or probe issues.	Student includes citations and extrapolates to informed opinions.	Student is willing to motivate and communicate with team members outside of class.	Student intentionally models professional behaviors with the goal of elevating class productivity.
Student appropriately shares views on evidence drawn from experience and legitimate resources.	Student can synthesize different points of view.	Student accepts feedback and revises work with a willingness to improve thinking, speaking, and writing.	Student exercises quality control and communicates expectations to research group members.	Student offers to write or rewrite assignments and posts revised work for online access by classmates.

Image Management	Seminar Discussion	Assignments	Leadership	Above and Beyond
Student is conscientious about improving their articulation of ideas and stays on point.	Student links current status of project to information and comments in previous classes.	Student is prepared for presentations.	Student identifies the strengths and weaknesses of team members.	Student speaks with teacher to request personal feedback for improvement.
Student informs teacher and team leader, in advance of conflicts, tardiness, missed deadline(s), or absence(s).	Student improves public speaking by addressing questions and comments to the entire class.	Student practices for presentations and understands material well enough to comment on and contextualize content.	Student chooses the best people for the job at hand, based on volunteers and requests for work.	Student increases class/research roles over time.

* ELL—English Language Learners

Team Leadership Rubric

Commitment	Integrity	Leadership	Responsibilities
Does what is best for the *TfC* learning community. Can be counted on to attend all classes and events. Notifies teacher and classmates if unable to do so.	Honest and fair in all dealings with others.	Strives to understand others and prioritizes developing strong relationships.	Leads by example and models professional behaviors.
Consistent, strong work ethic, completes work independently and works to ensure that teamwork outcomes are of consistently high quality.	Gives credit for work done by others whether verbally or in writing.	Provides enthusiastic support and encouragement to research group members.	Develops a strong relationship with the teacher and other adults.
Takes on additional roles/ assignments. Seeks help when needed.	Exhibits predictable, disciplined emotions and behaves with respect and good manners.	Brings research team together when a challenge must be met or has occurred	Brings research teammates' concerns to the teacher's attention.
Demonstrates a consistent commitment to self and team improvement.	Strives to develop strong relationships with teachers, fellow students and community members and professionals.	Demonstrates openness and creativity in the service of team cohesion and problem-solving approaches.	Is personally committed to realizing the aspirations and expectations of the lab.
Responsive to the needs of the *TfC* learning community and teammates. Takes responsibility for own actions.	Communicates appropriately to teammates, teachers, and professionals.	Listens to new and different ideas	Represents their school with respect and dignity.

Notes

Preface

1. A Duke University summer program that places undergraduates with Dublin-based NGOs and governmental organizations focused on, and often directed by, migrants and refugees. The students are asked to do the impossible: (1) "get" the culture of the organization and the people they work with well enough so they become "part of the family" and thus and have the privilege of (2) use their talents and gifts to help the organizations address challenges that are so significant they are often unstated.

2. Regents exams are required by New York State Department of Education as a high school graduation requirement.

3. J. S. Renzulli and S. M. Reis, *The Schoolwide Enrichment Model: A Comprehensive Plan for Educational Excellence* (Mansfield Center, CT: Creative Learning Press, 1985).

Introduction

1. We wish to acknowledge the College Board, Seminar for accurately framing research skills and proficiencies that are the focus of all social science research. See, for example, https://apcentral.collegeboard.org/courses/ap-seminar/course.

2. Here, as elsewhere in this book, we have found Tina Blythe et al., *The Teaching for Understanding Guide* (San Francisco, CA: Josey-Bass, 1998) to be a model for the organization of this book.

3. Martha Stone Wiske (Ed.), *Teaching for Understanding* (San Francisco, CA: Josey-Bass, 1998) and Grant Wiggins and Jay McTighe, *Understanding by Design* (Alexandria, VA: ASCD, 2005).

Step 1

1. Examples of how students and teachers have completed this inventory may be found in the resources page of the *TfC* website.

2. Haverford College has expanded on Kohlberg's classic dilemma structure with some contemporary dilemmas for young people, and this example is drawn from that collection, which can be found at http://ww3.haverford.edu/psychology/ddavis/p109g/kohlberg.dilemmas.html.

3. We have altered this dilemma slightly to conform to our needs.

Step 2

1. Sendhi Mullainatahn (Roman Family University Professor of Computation and Behavioral Science at University of Chicago), *The Ezra Klein Show* [Audio podcast], June 2019.

2. Larissa MacFarquhar, "What Money Can Buy," *New Yorker*, January 2016, 38.

3. While there are certainly some grammatical issues in the example above, the thinking that the students have done is impressive. The students narrowed their focus appropriately and identified an important relationship from which a question emerged that would be feasible for the class to research. This kind of thinking and doing is our goal in this step.

Step 5

1. This paragraph was informed by the code of ethics for the American Sociological Association. American Sociological Association, *Code of Ethics* (2018), https://www .asanet.org/sites/default/files/asa_code_of_ethics-june2018.pdf.

2. We advise examining only the general principles in professional codes of conduct, for example, pages 4–6 in the *Code of Ethics* for the American Sociological Association.

3. The elaborateness of this code of ethics is due to the fact that this research was conducted in a university setting and was undertaken to contribute to knowledge and thus needed to be approved by Duke Internal Review Board (IRB).

4. All research involving human subjects must be conducted in an ethical manner and with respect for participants. *TfC* research is designed to address challenges that concern the students who are participating and thus are particular to the communities in which the students live. *TfC* is not intended to develop or contribute to generalizable knowledge. If your research is intended to improve the community, it most likely does not have to be submitted to, or approved by, an IRB.

5. For example, if researchers ask people if they have committed illegal or criminal acts, they may be placing them at legal risk. Researchers have a clear obligation to inform human subjects of these risks. Again, we never ask these kinds of questions and urge you not to do so.

Step 6

1. Here are some common everyday data that you can use to practice data analysis: the comments sections under a news article, reviews of restaurants and hotels on Trip Advisor, Letters home from soldiers, New Deal Era Speeches, Descriptions of War, and any number of surveys and responses available online.

Step 7

1. Each year, college admissions directors from across the country receive many applications from high school students detailing how they created their *very own* tutoring program. In many cases, the applicants simply created another, often competing, program in a community that already had multiple tutoring programs. In conversations with these students when they reached college, Bill has learned that they realized it was easier to create a brand-new tutoring program than to undertake the hard and slow work of developing relationships with those who ran existing programs to see what gaps there were in the existing network—such as a shortage of mentoring programs for, and outreach in, refugee communities. Serious community challenges rarely get addressed by creating an array of similar and often competing programs that don't recognize one another.

2. For more information on this project, see Suzanne Shanahan and William Tobin, "Moral Purpose and Newcomer Youth: Cultivating Resilience Through Active Citizenship," *Social Education* 83, no. 6 (Nov/Dec 2019).

3. Produced by William Brakewood, Adena Kibel, Michael Mariam, David Rosenberg, Michael Sposato, William Tobin, and the Town of Rye, Tools for Change team.

4. We surveyed more than 200 high school students in the area and conducted five in-depth interviews with employers. We found that students have trouble finding jobs because they don't know what employers are looking for when making hiring decisions. The hints above are drawn from what employers from a range of businesses in the area told us they are looking for. These hints are also supported by much other research.

5. Rebecca Mead, "The Cinematic Traumas of Kenneth Lonergan," *New Yorker,* November 2016, https://www.newyorker.com/magazine/2016/11/07.

Appendix A

1. Adapted from The Self-Assessment Rubric Elements, created by Susan Saltrick and Valerie Feit. Not for reproduction (2007).

Index

Action Research for Community Change, 115–116
American Sociological Association, 135nn1–2
Analysis. *See* Data analysis
Arcaro, Greg, 48
Assessment, xxiv–xxx
  conversation, 51–54
  data analysis, 101–104
  data collection, 87–88
  design, 67–68
  knowledge implementation, 123–126
  perspective, 17–19
Awareness, 3–4

Beliefs, 9. *See also* Ethical reasoning
Bias, 5–6
The Brookings Institute, 41

Career Technical Education (CTE) program, 3
Case study
  conversation, 35–37
  data analysis, 91–92
  data collection, 71–73
  design, 56–57
  perspective, 3–4
  research questions, 22–24
Checklist, 102, 124. *See also* Teacher assessment
  for effective research questions, 30
Circumstances and constraints, 84–85
Civics classes, 33
Code names, 96
Code of ethics, 75–76
Code of Ethics (American Sociological Association), 135nn1–2
Coding, xviii, 96–97, 100–101
Cognitive skills, 129

Communication skills, 128–129
Community
  ethics and, 14–15
  problem solving, 117–118
  relationships and collaboration, 116–117
Community centers, xx
Community leaders, 23, 26. *See also* Conversation
Community organizations, building relationships with, 116–117, 126
Conclusion section of literature reviews, 47, 49
Confidentiality, 20, 31
Consent. *See* Informed consent
Constraints. *See* Circumstances and constraints
Content knowledge, 128
Conversation, xvi–xvii, 35–55
  assessment, 51–54
  case study, 35–37
  frequently asked questions, 54–55
  key features, 37–38
  planning, 38–49
  teaching, 50–51
Critical thinking strategies, 14
CTE. *See* Career Technical Education (CTE) program
Culture, 4
Curricular assessment, xxv–xxvi
  conversation, 53–54
  data analysis, 103–104
  data collection, 88
  knowledge implementation, 125–126
  perspective, 19
  research questions, 33
Curriculum, xiv–xv
  empirical research in, 64–66
  integrating ethical perspectives into, 14–16

Dalio, Ray, xxii
Data analysis, xvii–xviii, 90–105
  assessment, 101–104
  case study, 91–92
  frequently asked questions, 104–105
  goal of, 92
  key features, 92–93
  planning, 93–100
  teaching, 100–101
Databases, conversations with, 41–44
Data collection, xvii, 25, 71–89
  assessment, 87–88
  case study, 71–73
  frequently asked questions, 88–89
  in-depth interview, 61
  key features, 73–74
  methods, 60–61, 71–73
  participant observation, 60–61
  planning, 74–86
  survey, 60
  teaching, 86
DBQs (document-based questions), 38
Debate, 15–16
Decision-making, 15
Decisions, design, 59–62
Deductive planning approach, 50
Deep listening, 93
Deliberative design, 58–59
Design, xvii, 56–70
  assessment, 67–68
  case study, 56–57
  deliberative, 58–59
  frequently asked questions, 68–70
  key features, 57–58
  planning, 58–66
  teaching, 66–67
Discussion section of literature reviews,
    47–49
Distinctive individual perspectives, 5, 8–9

Effective research questions, 28–30
  checklist for, 30
  interest issues and, 29
  practice template, 30
Emotional skills. See Social and emotional skills
Empirical research. See Research
Engaged proactive attitude toward the world.
    See Proactive engagement
English (ELA) classes, xix, 33
Essential questions, 46
Ethical codes. See Code of ethics

Ethical obligation, xiii
Ethical perspective, xii–xiii, 12–16
Ethical questions, 16. See also Research
    question
Ethical reasoning, xiii, 9–17
Ethical reflection, 11–12
Evaluation of student's learning, 125

Ferraro, Barbara, 115
Fiction writing, perspective in, 19
Field notes, 96
Five-Step Techniques, 98–100
Flexibility, 120
Focus group, xxvi, 24, 41, 44, 57–58, 60
  conducting, 72–73, 81, 82–84
  creating effective prompts, 62–63
  data analysis, 95–98
  issues to be considered, 63
  note taking, 83
  organizing room, 83–84
  script, 82–83
Ford Foundation, 27
Formative assessment, xxv, xxvii–xxviii
  conversation, 51–52
  data analysis, 101–102
  data collection, 87
  design, 67
  knowledge implementation, 123–124
  perspective, 17–18
Four-Step Analysis Technique, 96–97, 102
Framing questions, 27–32
  curating challenge of, 30–32
  effective questions, 28–30
  techniques, 28
  trade-offs, 28
Freedom, 12
Frequently asked questions
  conversation, 54–55
  data analysis, 104–105
  data collection, 88–89
  design, 68–70
  knowledge implementation, 126
  research questions, 33–34

Google Forms, 85
Google spreadsheet, 101
Great Depression, 56, 78
Group performance
  conversations, 53
  data analysis, 103
  design, 68

knowledge implementation, 124
  perspective, 18–19
Group performance tasks, 68

Habits of mind, 129
Hall, Edward T., 4
High schools, assessment in, xxvii
Historical perspectives, 19

"I am" statements, 4
Identification of puzzles/problems, 26–27
Implementation of new knowledge. *See*
      Knowledge implementation
Implied consent, 78. *See also* Informed consent
Independent Learner Program (ILP), 116
In-depth interview, 61, 65–66. *See also*
      Interviews
Individual performance
  conversations, 52–53
  data analysis, 103
  design, 68
  perspective, 19
Individual perspective, 5. *See also* Perspective
  distinctive, 5, 8–9
  self-inventory, 8–9
Information skills, 128–129
Informed consent, 73–74
  implied consent, 78
  obtaining, 76–79
  purpose to be explained, 77
  reasons to participation, 77
  verbal consent, 78
  written consent, 78–79
Integrity, data collection with, 74
Internet, xiii–xiv, 90
Internship program, 121–122
Interpersonal skills. *See* Social and emotional
      skills
Interviews, xxix, 19, 22, 24–25, 81–82
  data analysis, 95–98
  in-depth, 61, 65–66
  issues to be considered, 63
  opening script, 82
  protocol, 81–82
Introduction section of literature reviews, 47

Job search, 119–120
JSTOR, 41

Kahane, Adam, 93
Kahneman, Daniel, xxii

Keeping record, 85–86
Kenan Institute for Ethics at Duke University,
      xii, 30
Key features
  conversation, 37–38
  data analysis, 92–93
  data collection, 73–74
  design, 57–58
  knowledge implementation, 111–112
  perspective, 5–6
  research questions, 24–25
Knowledge implementation, xviii, 106–126
  assessment, 123–126
  case studies, 106–111
  frequently asked questions, 126
  key features, 111–112
  planning, 112–122
  teaching, 122–123
Kohlberg Dilemma, 10, 134n2

Letter to an organization, 124
Listening, 92, 93
  deep, 93
  for understanding, 94–95
Literature, meaning of, 38
Literature reviews, 38, 39
  conclusion section, 47, 49
  discussion section, 47–49
  introduction section, 47
  social studies, 53–54
  structure, 45–47

Mental engagement, 7. *See also* Proactive
      engagement
Mindset, xxiii, 74–75
Moral reasoning. *See* Ethical reasoning
Morrison, Toni, 5
Mullainatahn, Sendhi, 24–25

Network, 120
The New Yorker, 41
The New York Times, 41
Nonfiction writing, perspective in, 19
Nonprofit organizations, 117
Noodle Tools, 41, 45, 115
Note taking, 83

One Child Nation, 114
Online resources, 62–63
Online surveys, 57, 85
Op-ed piece, 124

Open-ended questions, 14, 37–38
Opening script of interviews, 82

Panel discussion, 124
Participant observation, 60–61
Participants, interactions with, 79–84
    communication, 80–81
    conducting focus group, 81, 82–84
    interviews, 81–82
Peer panel, 101–102
Performance tasks, 68
    conversation, 52–53
    data analysis, 103
    design, 68
    knowledge implementation, 124
    perspective, 19
Personal awareness. *See* Awareness
Personality, 120
Perspective, xvi, 3–21
    assessment, 17–19
    bias, 5–6
    case study, 3–4
    concept of, 5
    distinctive individual perspectives,
        5, 8–9
    engaged proactive attitude toward the world,
        6–7
    ethical reasoning, 9–17
    key features, 5–6
    personal awareness, 3–4
    planning, 6–9
    self-inventory, 8–9
    teaching, 16–17
Pew Research, 41
Planning
    conversation, 38–49
    data analysis, 93–100
    data collection, 74–86
    design, 58–66
    knowledge implementation, 112–122
    perspective, 6–9
    research questions, 26–32
Portfolio, 125
Presentation, 120
Proactive engagement, 5, 6–7
Problems, identification of. *See* Puzzles/
    problems, identification of
Project-based learning (PBL), xx
Puzzles/problems, identification of,
    26–27

Quantitative assessment, xxviii
Questions. *See* Frequently asked questions;
    research questions
Quiz, 67–68

Reasonable behavior, 10. *See also* Ethical reasoning
Record keeping, 85–86
Reflection. *See* Ethical reflection
Research, xx–xxiv
    code of ethics, 75–76
    content curriculum, 64–66
    conversation. *See* Conversation
    data analysis. *See* Data analysis
    data collection. *See* data Collection
    design. *See* Design
    facilitation, xxiii–xxiv
    lab, xxii
    mindset, xxiii, 74–75
    perspective. *See* Perspective
    process, xxi–xxii
    as self-conscious/intentional investigation,
        xxi
    teams, xxiv
Research institutes, 41
Research papers, 45–46
    conclusion section, 47, 49
    discussion section, 47–49
    introduction section, 47
    structure of, 46–49
Research questions, xvi, xxv–xxvi
    assessment, 32–33
    case study, 22–24
    checklist for, 30
    conversation and, 40–41
    effective, 28–30
    framing, 27–28
    frequently asked questions, 33–34
    identifying puzzles and problems, 26–27
    key features, 24–25
    planning, 26–32
    practice template, 30
    relationship between interest issues and, 29
    strategies to develop, 31
    teaching, 32
Responses, grouping similar, 96
Responsibility/responsible decision, 10–11.
    See also Ethical reasoning
Responsible action/decisions, 10–11
Review, 38. *See also* Literature reviews
Rubrics, 18, 128–130

Santos, Nikolay, 4
Schoolwide Enrichment Model (SEM), 115
School-work-career research project, 4
Scientific American, 41
Script
    focus group, 82–83
    interview, 82
Seeing and Being Research Mindset, xxiii
Self-assessment, xxvii–xxviii, 125. *See also*
        Assessment
    conversation, 51
    data collection, 87
    design, 67
    perspective, 17–18
    rubrics, 18, 128–130
Self-inventory, 8–9
Self-regulation. *See* Social and emotional skills
Sense of identity, xiv
Service-learning projects (SLP), xx
Social and emotional skills, 129–130
Social movement, 125–126
Social science research. *See* Research
Solving Tough Problems (Kahane), 93
Sources
    conversation with. *See* Conversation
    truthfulness of, 39–40
South Africa, post-apartheid society, 93
Student Self-Assessment Rubric, 18, 128–130
Summative assessment, xxviii–xxx
    conversation, 52–53
    data analysis, 103
    data collection, 87–88
    design, 67–68
    knowledge implementation, 125
    perspective, 19
Survey, 60, 72
    administering, 72
    issues to be considered, 63
    questions, 62–63
    responses, analysis of, 95, 98–100
Survey Monkey, 85

Teacher assessment, xxviii. *See also* Assessment
    conversation, 52

data analysis, 102
data collection, 87
knowledge implementation, 124
perspective, 18
Teaching
    conversation, 50–51
    data analysis, 100–101
    data collection, 86
    design, 66–67
    knowledge implementation, 122–123
    perspective, 16–17
    research questions, 32
Technology skills, 128–129
Tetlock, Philip, xxii
Textual responses, analysis of, 95–98
    four-step analysis technique, 96–97
TfC. See Tools for Change (*TfC*)
Thomas, Dave, 48
Tools for Change (*TfC*), xii–xxx
    curricular integration, xix–xx
    curriculums and, xiv–xv
    guidebook, xv–xvi
    inquiry steps, xviii
    sense of identity, xiv
    steps, xv–xx. *See also Specific* step
    students' online engagement and, xiii–xiv
    usage, xviii–xix
Trade-offs, 28
Transitional thinking, 50
Truthfulness of sources, 39–40

Unconscious bias, 5–6
University lab, assessment in, xxvi–xxvii
"Uprooted/Rerouted," 75

Verbal consent, 78. *See also* Informed consent
Virtue, 12

Wang, Nanfu, 114
Welfare, 12
Westchester Joint Water Works (WJWW), 40
Work habits. *See* Social and emotional skills
Written consent, 78–79. *See also* Informed
        consent

About the Authors

William Tobin was born in Dublin, Ireland. He is a civil rights attorney and a research fellow at Duke University. At Duke, he created (with Suzanne Shanahan) the Honors Program in the Department of Sociology and currently codirects the Citizenship Lab at the Kenan Institute for Ethics. His teaching experiences ranges from directing PhD students to teaching kindergartners to tie their shoes. He has written on U.S. history, social science, and educational reform. He lives in Durham, North Carolina.

Valerie Feit was born in Johannesburg, South Africa. She is co-director of school counseling and K–12 enrichment coordinator at the Rye Neck School District in Mamaroneck, New York, where she specializes in building project-based learning programs, educational advisement, and the college process. Valerie was formerly a professional dancer who has toured internationally and she continues to work on dance performance and video projects in New York City. Valerie lives in Beacon, New York.